An Anthology

of East African

Poetry

EDITED BY

A. D. AMATESHE

 LONGMAN

I want to write a poem
a poem with a message
embellished with
images
symbols
subtle allusions
which even critics and poets
let aside other readers
will read and re-read
teasing their brains with wonder and thought
giving learned interpretations
in search of my 'original' meaning.

(Karamagi)

This anthology is dedicated to my sons,
Aloyo, Kuboka and Mandela; my daughter, Khamaya,
and all their future contemporaries; and to
my fellow strugglers in the understanding and
appreciation of poetry.

A. A.

Pearson Education Limited,
Edinburgh Gate, Harlow,
Essex CM20 2JE, England
and Associated Companies throughout the world.

First published 1988
Eight impression 2011

Set in 9/11pt Palatino
Printed in Malaysia, PPSB

ISBN 978-0-582-89522-5

Contents

Acknowledgements   vi
Introduction   1

PART ONE

When I see the beauty on my beloved's face Okot   18
p'Bitek (Uganda)
Beloved of my mother Okot p'Bitek (Uganda)   19
A Homecoming Kalungi Kabuye (Uganda)   19
Destiny Philippa Namutebi Barlow (Uganda)   20
Beloved E. H. S. Barlow (Uganda)   21
The Disabled Bangirana B-T. Kanzira Rwandambwe   22
(Uganda)
The end begins: words Kalungi Kabuye (Uganda)   23
I will cling to your garment Eric S. Ng'maryo (Tanzania)   24
The Analogy Bahadur Tejani (Tanzania)   25
Ploughing Noah K. Ndosi (Tanzania)   26
Message bearer Noah K. Ndosi (Tanzania)   27
A fight of roosters Noah K. Ndosi (Tanzania)   28
The Stubborn One Noah K. Ndosi (Tanzania)   29
Illegal Brew Noah K. Ndosi (Tanzania)   31
After the rains Noah K. Ndosi (Tanzania)   32
Song of the Worker E. Songoyi (Tanzania)   33
Turn-boy Richard S. Mabala (Tanzania)   35
Where are those songs? Micere Githae Mugo (Kenya)   37
Despair Edwin Waiyaki (Kenya)   39
Their City Lennard Okola (Kenya)   41
Extensions Humphrey Webuye (Kenya)   42
Come, My Mother's Son Lillian Ingonga (Kenya)   44
Betrothed Obyero Odhiambo (Kenya)   45
Witness Obyero Odhiambo (Kenya)   46

iii

Wedding eve Everett Standa (*Kenya*) 47
The Moslem Grave-Digger Jared Angira (*Kenya*) 49
Braying on and on . . . Jared Angira (*Kenya*) 50
At your feet Musaemura Bonas Zimunya (*Zimbabwe*) 51
An African Thunderstorm David Rubadiri (*Malawi*) 52
Yet Another Song David Rubadiri (*Malawi*) 53

PART TWO

Serenade Philippa Namutebi Barlow (*Uganda*) 56
Second burial Ejiet Komolo (*Uganda*) 57
Horizons Kalungi Kabuye (*Uganda*) 57
The Deep Freezer Richard S. Mabala (*Tanzania*) 58
Vicious Circle Makando Mandia (*Tanzania*) 59
The Bored Wife Freddy Macha (*Tanzania*) 60
Back Home Jwani Mwaikusa (*Tanzania*) 61
A Writer's Poem Innocent Karamagi (*Tanzania*) 62
Facelift For Kafira Francis Imbuga (*Kenya*) 63
Drowned in the Murmuring Crowd A. D. Amateshe 64
(*Kenya*)
At A Zebra Crossing A. D. Amateshe (*Kenya*) 65
Nyalgunga A. D. Amateshe (*Kenya*) 66
A Johannesburg Miner's Song Geoffrey K. King'ei 69
(*Kenya*)
Let Us Talk Together Everett Standa (*Kenya*) 70
A Pregnant School Girl Everett Standa (*Kenya*) 71
Conversation on African names Everett Standa (*Kenya*) 72
Important Things First, Dearest Arthur Luvai (*Kenya*) 73
The Death of My Father Henry Indangasi (*Kenya*) 74
Like the Sea and its Waters Waigwa Wachira (*Kenya*) 75
Ngoma Yusuf O. Kassam (*Kenya*) 77
Fort Jesus Amin Kassam (*Kenya*) 78
Kano Plains Robert Okinyi (*Kenya*) 79
The Dawn Lillian Ingonga (*Kenya*) 80
Women Walking At Alice and Trevor's Wedding Or 82
Intermarriage David Rubadiri (*Malawi*)
Death At Mulago David Rubadiri (*Malawi*) 83
He passes by me . . .! Felix Mnthali (*Malawi*) 84
Silence in the boardroom Felix Mnthali (*Malawi*) 85
Farewell to a Volkswagen Felix Mnthali (*Malawi*) 86

PART THREE

Twin Ceremony Richard Ntiru (*Uganda*) 90
The function Richard Ntiru (*Uganda*) 91

Rhythm of the pestle Richard Ntiru (*Uganda*)   92
The Guilt of Giving Laban Erapu (*Uganda*)   94
A Taxi Driver on his Death Timothy Wangusa (*Uganda*)   95
I Met a Thief Austin Bukenya (*Uganda*)   96
The Struggle Kalungi Kabuye (*Uganda*)   97
Rain David Kihazo (*Uganda*)   98
Lead Kindly Dark David Kihazo (*Uganda*)   99
Not All At Once David Kihazo (*Uganda*)   99
The Motoka Theo Luzuka (*Uganda*)   101
To the Childless Kittobbe (*Uganda*)   102
Being John Ruganda (*Uganda*)   103
Brotherly Advice Raymond Ntalindwa (*Rwanda*)   104
The Money-Changers Richard S. Mabala (*Tanzania*)   105
Question Richard S. Mabala (*Tanzania*)   106
The Ways Of The World Richard S. Mabala (*Tanzania*)   107
Groaning for Burial Felix Mnthali (*Malawi*)   108
A Leopard Lives in a Muu Tree Jonathan Kariara (*Kenya*)   110
The Desert Amin Kassam (*Kenya*)   112
Maji Maji Yusuf O. Kassam (*Kenya*)   113
Epistle to Uganda Leteipa Ole Sunkuli (*Kenya*)   114
The Ahs and Ohs of Admiration Kwendo Opanga   115
(*Kenya*)
Armanda Jared Angira (*Kenya*)   117
The final appeal Jared Angira (*Kenya*)   119
The letters Jared Angira (*Kenya*)   120
By the Seaside A. D. Amateshe (*Kenya*)   122
The Anniversary A. D. Amateshe (*Kenya*)   123
Mother of Children A. D. Amateshe (*Kenya*)   125
Flight No. BA-067 A. D. Amateshe (*Kenya*)   127
To the Shameless One Francis Imbuga (*Kenya*)   128

Glossary   130
Index of Poems by Author   134

Acknowledgements

The idea to produce this anthology began in 1985 during a course I was taking at the Institute of Education, University of London (U.K.). I would not have been able to realize this project had it not been for the inspiration I received from my loving wife, Rose Maleche.

I am also deeply grateful to the following individuals for their tremendous encouragement and contributions: Messrs. Francis Imbuga, Arthur Luvai, Geoffrey Kingei and Barasa Kukubo; Professors Matthew Maleche and David Rubadiri; Mrs Valery Kibera and Mrs Waveney Olembo; Dr Everett Standa, Mzee Daniel Kuboka and Mama Emily. All those who typed the manuscript, I sincerely acknowledge their sacrifice.

A. A.

The publishers would like to thank the following for permission to include copyright poems:

The author, A D Amateshe for his poems 'Drowned in the Murmuring Crowd', 'At a Zebra Crossing', 'Nyalgunga', 'By the Seaside', 'The Anniversary', 'Mother of Children' and 'Flight No BA-067'; the author, Jared Angira for his poems 'The Moslem Grave-Digger', 'Braying on and on', 'The letters' and 'The final appeal'; Edward Arnold, A Division of Hodder and Stoughton Ltd for an extract from pp 175–200 *The Practical Criticism of Poetry* by Cox and Dyson; the author, Philippa Namutebi Barlow for her poems 'Destiny' and 'Serenade'; the author, A S L Bukenya for his poem 'I Met a Thief'; Heinemann Educational Books Ltd for the poems 'When I see the beauty on my beloved's face' and 'Beloved of my mother' from *Horn Of My Love* by Okot p'Bitek; the author, Francis Imbuga for his poems 'To the Shameless One' and 'Facelift For Kafira'; Mr Francis Imbuga on behalf of the author, Leteipa Ole Sunkuli for his poem 'Epistle to Uganda'; the author Dr Henry Indangasi for his poem 'The Death of My Father' from *Mwangaza: Journal of the Literature Students Association* Vol 1, No 2, 1987; the author, Lillian Ingonga for her poems 'Come, My Mother's Son' and 'The Dawn'; the author, (Kabuto) Kalungi-Kabuye for his poems 'The end begins: words', 'Horizons' and 'A Homecoming'; the author, Innocent Karamagi, University of Dar es Salaam for his poem 'A Writer's Poem' © Innocent Karamagi; the author, Jonathan Kariara for his poem 'A Leopard Lives in a Muu Tree'; Kenya Literature Bureau for the poems 'Where are those songs?' by Micere Githae Mugo from pp 2–4 *Daughter Of My People, Sing*, 'Second burial' by Ejiet Komolo from p 54 *Dhana* Vol 3, No 2, 1973 and 'Twin Ceremony' by Richard Ntiru from p 37 *Dhana* Vol 3, No 2, 1973; the author, David Kihazo for his poems 'Rain', 'Lead Kindly Dark' and 'Not All At Once'; the author, Geoffrey K King'ei for his poem 'A Johannesburg Miner's Song'; Longman Group UK Ltd for the poems: 'Armanda' from *Cascades* by Jared Angira, 'Groaning for Burial', 'He passes by me . . .', 'Silence in the boardroom' and 'Farewell to a Volkswagen' by Felix Mnthali from pp 56–8, 51–2, 60 and & 86–9 *When Sunset Comes To Sapitwa* (1982) and 'At your feet' by Musaemura Bonas Zimunya from p 73 *Thought Tracks* (1982); the author, Arthur Luvai for his poem 'Important Things First, Dearest'; the author, R Mabala for his poems 'Turn-boy', 'Question', 'The Deep Freezer', 'The Ways of the World' and 'The Money-Changers'. R Mabala on behalf of F Macha for his poem 'The Bored Wife' and M E A Mandia for his poem 'Vicious Circle'; the author, Jwani Mwaikusa, University of Dar es Salaam for his poem 'Back Home' © Jwani Mwaikusa; the author, Dr Noah K Ndosi for his poems 'Ploughing', 'Message bearer', 'A fight of roosters', 'The Stubborn One', 'Illegal Brew' and 'After the rains'; the author, Raymond Ntalindwa for his poem 'Brotherly Advice'; Pergamon Books Ltd for the poems 'An African Thunderstorm' by David Rubadiri from *Pergamon Poets: Poetry From Africa* edited by H Sergeant and 'Yet Another Song' by David Rubadiri from *Pergamon Poets: Poetry From India* edited by H Sergeant; the author, David Rubadiri for his poems 'Women Walking At Alice and Trevor's Wedding Or Intermarriage' and 'Death At Mulago'; the author, John Ruganda for his poem 'Being' from pp 132–3 *Drum Beat* ed Okola (1967); the author, Bangirana B-T Kanzira Rwandambwe for his poem 'The Disabled'; Martin Secker & Warburg Ltd for the poems: 'The Struggle' by (Kabuto) Kalungi-Kabuye, 'The Desert' by Amin Kassam, 'Maji Maji' by Yusuf O Kassam, 'To the Childless' by Kittobbe, 'The Motoka' by Theo Luzuka and 'The Analogy' by Bahadur Tejani from *Poems From Black Africa* edited by Wole Soyinka; the author, E Songoyi, University of Dar es Salaam for his poem 'Song of the Worker'; the author, Professor E M Standa for his poems 'Wedding eve', 'Let Us Talk Together', 'A Pregnant School Girl' and 'Conversation on African names'; Tanzania Publishing House for the poem 'I will cling to your garment' by Eric Ng'maryo from *Summons: Poems For Tanzania* edited by R S Mabala (1980); the author, Dr T Wangusa for his poem 'A Taxi Driver on his Death'; the author, Humphrey O D Webuye for his poem 'Extensions'; the author, Kwendo Opanga Wellington for his poem 'The Ahs and Ohs of Admiration'.

We have been unable to trace the copyright holders in the following poems and would appreciate any information that would enable us to do so:

'Beloved' by E H S Barlow; 'The Guilt of Giving' by L Erapu from p 42 *Poem From East Africa* ed Cook & Rubadiri (Heinemann); 'Ngoma' by Yusuf O Kassam from p 81 *Poems From East Africa* ed Cook & Rubadiri (Heinemann); 'Like the sea and its Waters' by W Wachira; 'Their City' by Lennard Okola; 'Fort Jesus' by Amin Kassam from p 48 *Drum Beat* ed L Okola; 'Kano Plains' by Robert Okinyi from p 44 *Ghala* Vol 5, No 7 (July 1968); 'The function' and 'Rhythm of the pestle' by Richard Ntiru from pp 23 & 75 *Tensions* (1971); 'Despair' by Edwin Waiyaki from *Drum Beat* ed L Okola (1967).

Introduction

There have been a number of anthologies on East African poetry ever since writing in English gained momentum in Africa. Some of these anthologies have been a mere collection of poems without a supportive, comprehensive introduction to explain the purpose of the poems under study or to offer guidance to a keen reader. As a result, poetry has been seen by many as an exclusive occupation for those who perhaps have the talent to read between the lines, as it were. Many students in our secondary schools have, in fact, tended to shy away from any discussions relating to written poetry. The situation at the university has been no better. Students have tended to tackle novels or plays and the best they have done to poetry is mere recitation! There is no doubt that such relegation does harm to an otherwise very lively and creative literary field.

The poetry in this anthology has been carefully selected from individuals who have responded variously, in poetic terms, to common experiences in our part of the world. It was felt necessary to draw from as far as Malawi and Zimbabwe because of the need to compare our own responses to life with those of others who do not necessarily come from within East Africa. Above all, one purpose of this anthology, through its introduction, is to erase from our students' minds the misconception that poetry is a difficult field. They should instead realize that poetry is, in fact, a very enjoyable and nourishing area of study, not only for those faced with examinations in their literature courses but even for those who wish to relate themselves to the many facets of life as meaningfully as possible. In Kenya, where the 8-4-4 education system has now been introduced, this anthology will offer a particularly good start for those who wish to carry out further exploration in poetry at the university level. Some of the poems may already be familiar to the readers because they have appeared elsewhere in journals or other collections. This should not be seen as an unnecessary repetition or as a lack of initiative to explore 'virgin' land. Such poems were simply selected out of the editor's very deep respect for age and experience. Other poems may be totally unfamiliar from contributors who have not been heard of. The idea was to combine the old and the young, the archival and the new, the real and the absurd, so that we are exposed to a variety for purposes of comparison. Also, through this kind of arrangement, the aspiring poets have been offered an opportunity to stand alongside the well-known names.

We should now, at this stage, attempt to answer one recurrent question: *What is poetry?* Poetry is simply a form of expression, either oral or written. It is a form of communication between the artist and his audience or the reader. According to William Wordsworth, one of the early Romantic poets in Europe, 'a poet is a man speaking to his fellow men'. In other words, poetry is a form of speech, only that instead of being found in an ordinary setting, it is usually elevated to the realm of figurative language (that is, use of metaphors, similes and other related symbols) in order to enrich the normal manner of speech. According to Njuguna Mugo, to be of genuine use,

> poetry must articulate a people's collective experience; it must enrich the precious safe in which the sinews of the collective group are preserved. It is for this reason that the poet who puts a people's idiom and metaphor into poetic verse soon captures the imagination of his/her audience, soon gains central ground, because the artist becomes his/her people's collective articulation.[1]

Poetry, therefore, essentially offers an opportunity for shared experiences since it consists of spontaneous recollections which stir the emotions of the reader or the audience. And Richard Ntiru, one of the contributors to this anthology, says:

> The business of poetry in particular is to explore the numerous modes of human response to the problems inherent in a world that is naturally hostile and is increasingly becoming more and more complex in all its manifestations.[2]

Within this context, poetry can be seen as social commentary on individuals or society because of its economic use of words and also because of its use of appropriate imagery. In basic terms, poetry is music – particularly within oral situations – relying heavily on rhythm. In this way, it is 'singable' and even 'danceable', re-creating itself in the process. But it would be an insurmountable task for us to attempt an exhaustive definition of poetry. One however hopes that other definitions or aspects will emerge in the course of this anthology or in the course of other relevant discussions on the subject.

THE DIFFERENCE BETWEEN ORAL AND WRITTEN POETRY

When one considers the position of oral poetry in Africa, an obvious element that emerges is that this medium of expression takes the form of a collective activity. From time immemorial, it has been expressed at funerals, marriages, child-naming ceremonies and so on. An instant collective response is achieved because, generally, oral poetry is expressed through a language and an idiom which the entire community understands. Take the example of Okot p'Bitek's 'When I see the Beauty on my Beloved's face' which appears in this anthology. It is an oral love poem among the Acoli ethnic community of Northern Uganda which was translated from vernacular into English but which still retains its local appeal in terms of simplicity and the imagery used.

Written poetry is in fact a recent innovation in Africa and one which requires the participants to have acquired reading skills. In other words, literacy has resulted in the coexistence of oral and written forms. But we should always remember that the one form of art which still is accessible to a majority audience – the illiterate population – is the oral art form. It is for this reason that one is justified in regarding it as the most popular medium in Africa through which relevant, social comments are expressed. Also, its success is determined by the fact that it is able to involve a big population of the community since it assumes an oral delivery. The oral aspect puts the relevant public in a better position to participate and interpret a situation than would be the case in the written art form. For example, members of a particular society are able to share in an experience (be it funeral, marriage, circumcision or any other cultural activity) as emotionally as the occasion allows. Among the themes of the Acoli dirges, for instance, Okot p'Bitek cites incidents in which man's life is compared to vegetable leaves that soon wither and dry up:

3

> *Beloved of my mother*
> *is like plucked vegetable leaves . . .*
> *Death has destroyed a prince . . .*[3]

(This poem appears in this anthology under the title, 'Beloved of my mother').

One advantage with imagery such as the one above is that it would be understood by all those listening or reciting. Also, such words are repetitively sung or chanted in order to lay emphasis wherever it is due and in order to maximize the quality of collective response. In this respect, the oral art-form does not, by its very nature of delivery, become a monopoly of only a few individuals in society. The talented poet's creative response to a situation or an experience is like a stone gently thrown into a pool of water, whose spontaneous effect is to cause ripples throughout the water body. The impact is not the same once poetry becomes written.

The emergence of literacy in Africa has, therefore, meant major deviations from the oral art form into the written form. It has meant, for example, that poetry is written down by an individual who perhaps has the literate audience in mind. In this case, problems of the delivery of this written poetry to the audience arise. So far, there are perhaps only two ways: either it is read privately by those who have acquired reading abilities or it is *performed* to a largely non-reading audience. The latter is not yet a popular phenomenon in East Africa but one hopes that it will be taken up not only during festivals but also during other occasions in schools and elsewhere. However, one needs to bear in mind the fact that not all written poetry can be dramatized due to individual limitations in form and content. Oral poetry succeeds mainly because its performance is like a play on the stage with the audience watching it alive. The performer utilizes such paralinguistic features as body movements, gestures and facial expressions in order to engage the audience in the subject matter as vividly as possible. Indeed, as Isidore Okpewho says:

> Oral poetry achieves its forcefulness not only at the hands of the performer himself. Part of this forcefulness comes from the participation of various persons (present at the scene of performance) in the creative act taking place.[4]

A JUSTIFICATION FOR THIS ANTHOLOGY

The foregoing discussion seems to have heaped a lot of praise on oral poetry at the expense of what perhaps gives this anthology

4

its existence – written poetry. But under the above heading we shall generally analyse the social function of poetry in our modern times in order that the poems in this collection are seen as a valuable contribution to the world of creativity.

The uses of poetry certainly vary as society alters and as the public to be addressed changes. Indeed, poetry, through the various stages of Africa's history, has been meeting with new challenges. A good example is the poetry that was born out of the Negritude movement. There is a sense in which Negritudist poetry in its earlier stages followed, to a degree, the traditional pattern of a collective experience. Negritudist poets, whether they came from the Caribbean or Africa, had the same goal: the affirmation of the African personality, in cultural terms, before the white world. This was in reaction to white racism whose main objectives were to oppress and exploit while at the same time, discriminating against the black race. This kind of poetry which glorified the black man's cultural values served a very useful purpose at a time when all Africa was colonized. It contributed a lot to the morale of the struggle for independence right from the second quarter of this century. Indeed, Leopold Sedar Senghor defined negritude as the awareness, defence and development oi African cultural values.[5] The attack by black poets on the western values and the emphasis on oral traditions in Africa was viewed as the social function of poetry at that particular stage of Africa's history. Poetry was one of the instruments in the war of liberation and the poets saw no victory in this war without a cultural bias.

But the use of English or French by Africa's poets posed a language problem which greatly modified the ability of the poets to speak to or for the entire community. In any case, in the wake of independence in most of the African states, Negritudist poetry lost considerably in its social function because of the tendency to glorify Africa at the expense of the harsh realities of neocolonialism which were already gripping her. Lennard Okola, making specific reference to the East African situation, said:

> The East African poet seems, in his relative aloofness from Negritude enthusiasm, to be striving to come to grips with the present. Perhaps he feels, subconsciously, that much of the colonial situation has been explained away for him by the longer established West African poets, and, therefore considers Negritude a dead subject which would dissipate his creative energy in vague nostalgia.[6]

In other words, what Okola viewed as 'striving to come to grips with the present' may be interpreted as the new social role of East

5

African poetry – a conscious effort to comment about modern society and the experiences therein. There is no doubt that most of the poems in this anthology attempt to live up to this role. Our poets have certainly found some new grounds for poetic expression bearing in mind the fact that:

> The African (poet) can be successful if he is sufficiently sensitive towards his reading public, and employs themes that either have a significant bearing upon real life or give a clear insight into the nature and the general spirit of the age or society he is writing about.[7]

The new approaches in poetry have become necessary in keeping with the various modifications that have been taking place in our education systems. The main objective is to enable our students to adopt new skills in practical criticism and also to make them easily adaptable to their changing, immediate environments. With regard to the revised literature syllabuses, emphasis is now being laid more and more on language aspects. This is because we, the educationists, strongly believe that a student who has a good command of the language inevitably follows more clearly other aspects of the school curricula. This editor sincerely believes that the poetry in this anthology will give the student some necessary skills in language expression. Take the example of 'Ngoma' by Yusuf O. Kassam:

> *The drum beats,*
> *And with bare feet and red earth,*
> *Rhythm erupts,*
> *Muscles and drums synchronized.*

These are just the first four lines of the poem but a keen student should benefit with regard to the following: use of *precise* description, appropriate choice of words, meaningful relationship of images, vivid portrayal of an activity which the artist captures with his poetic eye, and noteworthy vocabulary such as the use of 'synchronized'. It should also be borne in mind that useful language acquisition depends very much on practice. The more practices or the more exposure a student has with various forms of expression, the more he will develop confidence and competence in language use. The poetry in this collection offers the necessary variety to the student. Nearly all the poems will, to some degree, stir the reader's emotions so that he/she is not just a *passive* observer but an *active* participant. In any case, poetry should really be seen as forms of conversations between the poet

6

and the reader or the audience. And, as is usual in every conversation, the one being talked to should pay close attention because all the time the speaker will be expecting some form of response. Take the example of Theo Luzuka's 'The Motoka':

> You see that Benz sitting at the rich's end?
> Ha! That motoka is motoka
> It belongs to the Minister for Fairness
> Who yesterday was loaded with a doctorate
> At Makerere with whisky and I don't know what
> Plus I hear the literate thighs of an undergraduate.

The whole poem is conversational and maximises the reader's involvement. It also shows the richness of language which modern written poetry seems to display — a form of expression which evidently is drawn from the ordinary everyday speech but which is flavoured through an appropriate choice of words in order to make an immediate impression on the reader. The subject matter is certainly not anything unfamiliar to the student but the poet's style should benefit the reader in terms of acquainting himself/herself with the use of *sarcasm* or *irony* and also with the increasing significance of *free verse* which has become typical of most modern African poetry.

It should also be noted that the appreciation of poetry is like partaking in a holy communion – the evaluation of taste depends very much on personal, past experience. In other words, students should be guided through the study of poetry bearing in mind not only their past knowledge or exposure but also the respective contexts of the material itself. Some of the poets whose work appears in this anthology have been accused of not living up to certain expectations. For instance, Ngugi wa Thiongo, at one stage, stated that:

> The poets (for example, David Rubadiri, Jonathan Kariara, Sam Mbure, Jared Angira, Richard Ntiru), like their counterparts in fiction, have not in the past sufficiently explored the technical resources of the oral tradition or realized that these can revitalize their poetry and enable them to move in a different direction.[8]

Aware of the spontaneity of any artistic work, it would be unfair to disregard any poetry whose creators have not perhaps fulfilled the above requirement by Ngugi. We should in fact remember that every artist (no matter the manner of expression) makes very useful contributions to the literary field and, in this way, he or she

7

enriches creativity by adding variety and novelty. It is true that we want our students to be aware of poets who have kept close to the African soil, as it were, and who therefore readily appeal to us through their themes and style. But we also want our students to know about 'private' poets whose works we must penetrate in order to pass judgement on who we think is most fit for our mutual, literary consumption.

CATEGORIES OF POETRY AND STYLE

By now students should have been made aware of the various categories of poetry in terms of some of the following topics: love, praise, mockery, politics, gods and ancestors, nostalgia, and so on. The categorization in this case largely depends on the subject matter of each poem. But one need not be rigid about this because certain poems fall in more than one category. This anthology has deliberately avoided the conventional approach in this regard so that the grouping or the classification of any poem becomes one of the tasks for the student. The teacher will be expected to provide guidance in cases where a student might find difficulty. For purposes of logical progression, the anthology has been divided into three main parts: Part One, Part Two and Part Three. Part One essentially consists of the easier poems which may fit quite conveniently in well-known oral contexts or which may simply provide a good beginning for the class. Part Two has the less easy ones which may perhaps offer a good challenge to students in Form 3 and above. Part Three consists of the more difficult poetry which is convenient for school candidates or beginners at the university level. The rationale behind this form of categorization was the view of the entire educational processes as a kind of ladder – one has to inevitably begin from the bottom rung and gradually work his or her way to the top.

In terms of style, the obvious form that emerges in this anthology is free verse which, by implication, is not tied to any conventional standards of metre form, rhyme scheme and stanza patterns. During colonial days, for example, and even after independence, most of the poetry found in schools was from the western world. The emphasis here was basically on the 'titam-titam-titi-tam-titam' patterns of rhythm. Metre and the rhyme schemes were stressed and one was labelled a good student depending on whether he or she read the poem correctly according to these sound arrangements. But now what has emerged out of Africa is a kind of poetry popularly referred to as 'free verse' but which, by all means, equally makes effective representation of a people's expression. Take the example of Richard S. Mabala's 'The Money-Changers':

> *Our Father who art in – CLINK –*
> *hallowed be thy – CLINK –*
> *Thy – CLINK – come*
> *Thy will be – CLINK –*
> *On earth as it is in heaven.*
> *Give us this day our daily – CLINK –*
> *And forgive us our – CLINK –*

The poet is not merely playing around with the word 'CLINK'. He is in fact making a very important point, through this *onomatopoeic* usage, about modern churches which have become money-makers instead of their traditional role as providers of spiritual satisfaction. The churches have become exploitative and what the poet does is to introduce a new style in order to describe more emphatically the nature of exploitation. Or take the example of Yusuf O. Kassam's 'Maji Maji':

> *Placing both his hands on his head,*
> *He looked down on the earth and pronounced,*
> *"They fired bullets, not water, no, not water."*
> *He looked up, with a face crumpled with agony,*
> *And with an unsteady swing of his arm, he said,*
> *"Dead, we all lay dead". (lines 21–26).*

In this poem, the poet has introduced the use of dialogue and achieves a conversational tone. There is also no doubt that, through this method, both the narrator and his listeners relate to each other quite closely. One also notices the use of *repetition* in the third line of the quoted section above for purposes of emphasis. There is also the use of *paradox* in the last line to bring out the catastrophic nature of the Maji Maji Rebellion during the colonial days. On the surface level, the whole poem may be regarded as a piece of prose but on a deeper level it has a poetic form which is quite intense and appealing. One last example in this discussion of style is Dr Everett Standa's 'Wedding eve':

> *Should I*
> *Or should I not*
> *Take the oath to love*
> *For ever*
> *This person I know little about?*

9

Does she love me
Or my car
Or my future
Which I know little about?

Will she continue to love me
When the future she saw in me
Crumbles and fades into nothing
Leaving the naked me
To love without hope? (lines 1–14)

The poet here is in conversation with himself. He is expressing his fears about marriage and the uncertainty with which man and woman take each other to the altar for matrimony. But Standa is doing it in an enquiring or questioning way. In other words, he is posing *rhetorical* questions which do not necessarily require immediate answers but which give the reader an opportunity to reflect upon the issues the poet is raising.

From the examples so far discussed it is clear that artists use various styles to express themselves. Students should be encouraged in identifying as many of these as possible beginning from fundamental questions. What kind of expression does the poet use? What is the significance or what are the special features of the language used? In what way(s) does the poem make an impact upon the reader or the audience? Students must all the time recognize the interdependence of **form** and **content** so that aspects of style are given as much weight as the themes themselves. We also need to be quite clear on the components of style itself, for example, use of contrast or juxtaposition; use of figurative language (imagery, symbolism, and so on); use of setting or background; use of repetition; use of irony and sarcasm; use of lyrical elements; use of personification; use of allegory or allusions; use of sibilance or alliteration or onomatopoeia; use of hyperbole; use of paradox; use of monologue and dialogue. There are several others. Most of the ones mentioned are aspects that the students are likely to encounter in this anthology, hopefully with the guidance of their teachers. Some of the questions at the end of respective poems have, in fact, specifically addressed themselves to these elements so that students can acquire a balanced approach, in both thematic and stylistic terms, to the interpretation of poetry.

THE TEACHING OF POETRY IN SCHOOLS

Over the years poetry has not quite received the kind of attention it deserves in the school curricula. In most cases, written poetry has been set aside as exclusive to those students who major in literature. Ironically, however, schools have been very keen with their entries into annual music festivals and most of them have won commendable awards in these competitions. Students, on their part, have been quite innovative with their own original compositions during such sessions. Yet we, the teachers, have not done our best to make them realize the close link there is between these forms of expressions and the written poetry which they tend to shun. Effective teaching of poetry in our schools should in fact begin from the experiences the students themselves gain from these music festivals because, as we stated earlier, poetry is music. By relating to oral poetry, the students are able to begin from the known to the unknown. They are able to recapture the vividness of the environments within which they grow and, above all, they are able to creatively find answers to the following crucial questions posed by Micere Githae Mugo's 'Where are those songs?'

Where are those songs
my mother and yours
always sang
fitting rhythms
to the whole
vast span of life?

What was it again
they sang
            harvesting maize, threshing millet, storing the grain . . .
What did they sing
bathing us, rocking us to sleep . . .
and the one they sang
stirring the pot
(swallowed in parts by choking smoke)?   *(lines 1–14)*

With the above in mind, our interpretation of poetic expressions should necessarily begin from our traditional backgrounds and then gradually delve into other forms. The emphasis, in these initial stages, must be on group performances or discussions. Even when the poem in question appears to have been written in a secluded poetic world, we must always make every attempt to bring it down to earth, as it were, through motivated class discussions. In order to achieve this one must always be quite careful about the choice of poems to be discussed. One hopes that this choice is made as objectively as possible and that one of the criteria should be whether it can make exciting and yet thought provoking reading for the student. Listen, for example, to the

11

following dance poem on Rumba and let us see if we cannot in fact all march together in the appreciation of poetry as a great source of inspiration:

> Zumba, mama, la rumba y tambo!
> Mabimba, mabomba, mabomba y bombo!
> Buzzling mama, the rumba with its drum!
> Mabimba, mabomba, mabimba, kong-kong.
> She dances the rumba, the blackish Tomasa,
> He dances the rumba, Josè Encarnacion!
> She's rolling her right hip, she's rolling her left hip,
> He turns and he squats and he jerks his behind,
> He pushes his belly, he bows and he marches
> On one of his heels, and one drags behind.
> Chaqui, chaqui, chaqui, chaqui,
> Chaqui, chaqui, chaqui, chaqui![9]

Here is a poem that is dramatic and one which should obviously appeal to a beginner. It is full of action, lends itself to performance, and draws from relevant aspects of any oral tradition – that is, song and dance. Needless to say, the above poem, if introduced in a classroom situation, ought to be read aloud (which should also be the case for *all* poems) so that its total effect is realized. In the case of this poem, the rhythm is represented by the 'chaqui, chaqui, chaqui, chaqui' of the last lines. It is an onomatopoeic usage to highlight the sound of *maraccas*, which are the gourd rattles used as musical accompaniment. If a teacher can successfully act this poem in class, it can neither be long before the students enthusiastically join in nor before they too struggle to create something of their own.

It is true that the modern artist, in as far as his relationship with the audience remains vaguely defined, cannot uphold the accountability of the oral poet who has always functioned as:

> the record of experience of his society, and as the
> voice of vision in his own time.[10]

It is therefore expected that teachers of literature play the role of mediator between the written poetry and those who study it so that some kind of rapport is established. It is the teachers' responsibility to mould a habitable, poetic world not only for a small minority but for a large section of students who go through our school systems. The foundation we lay in Forms 1 and 2 will determine the response we get in Forms 3 and 4 and beyond. As stated earlier, we must therefore begin from the simplest of the collection of poems at hand to the most difficult; we must begin from the most familiar, slowly building up to the most unusual. Take the example of Obyero Odhiambo's 'Betrothed':

> *The bride they said*
> *had gone through school*
> *primary secondary university upwards:*
> *Three thousand shillings is not enough.*
>
> *For having fed her*
> *   schooled her*
> *   employed her*
> *Three thousand shillings is not enough –*   *(lines 1–8)*

This poem is quite simple and is humorously presented. The subject matter is dowry discussions and the conversation between the girl's parents and the intending suitor is made much more real by the choice of familiar words and expressions. No reader should have any problem at all in grasping the content of this poem. Another good example of this kind of simplicity is Lilian Ingonga's 'Come, My Mother's Son':

> *Come, my mother's son*
> *You're no longer a baby*
> *Stop following the women*
> *To the firesides*
> *Stop peeping in the cooking pot*
> *Stop pinching the girls*
> *You're no longer a baby*
> *You are a man.*   *(lines 1–8)*

Apart from its admirable simplicity, this poem is also *didactic*. It teaches the young boys how to fit into society and states in cultural terms, what is expected of them. In other words, it stresses the qualities which make a man by advising the boy – 'my mother's son' – to keep away from the cooking place and from the women. The rest of the poem clearly deals with the division of labour between girls and boys when they are growing up together in a homestead or in a village. Such themes are drawn from the students' immediate environments and so they make a spontaneous appeal particularly to those who might be encountering written poetry for the first time.

But, admittedly, there are some difficult areas in poetry which need to be approached quite cautiously. There is no fixed formula as to how one can interpret such poetry except that one needs to begin by very careful reading, seeing the lines in the poem as inter-related and trying to make meaning out of the many parts of the piece of work. A dictionary ought to be used in cases where difficult words have been employed so that more light is thrown into the dark areas of the poem. In instances where vernacular words have been used (because possibly they couldn't be translated into English) and no explanations have been given by the poet, a student needs to make do with the impressions he or she might form from certain clues within the poem. From this discussion one already sees that the study of poetry is an exercise that requires patience and tolerance. It also requires a student to be firmly acquainted with a wide variety of language use so that he or she can deal with poetic tasks with speed and reasonable accuracy. Take the example of Jonathan Kariara's 'A Leopard Lives in a Muu Tree':

> A leopard lives in a Muu tree
> Watching my home
> My lambs are born speckled
> My wives tie their skirts tight
> And turn away –
> Fearing mottled offspring.   (lines 1–6)

We should remember that in every work of art, there is the *literal* level and the *symbolic* level. The literal level in the above poem would simply be referring to the owner of a homestead and the fear he has about the safety of his lambs (sheep) because of the leopard which lives in a nearby 'muu' (fig) tree. But then the idea of his wives comes in and so we move from the literal level to the symbolic level and examine much more keenly some of the sexual images the poem evokes. It turns out that the leopard is in fact an outsider (possibly a neighbour) who takes advantage of the speaker's implied sexual weakness to 'cohabit' with his wives. These extramarital relationships result in 'speckled' or 'mottled' offspring, very much resembling the 'leopard' – an indication of his having fathered 'coloured' children from the man's wives. And now the speaker says of the leopard and of himself:

> He peers at me with slit eyes
> His head held high
> My sword has rusted in the scabbard.   (line 19–21)

The confession contained in the last line above makes us now understand why the man wishes to cut down the 'muu' tree as a way of getting rid of the leopard. He is obviously full of anger for the intruder and at the same time we feel pity for him when he implies that what has incapacitated him, in sexual terms, is old age:

> *My fences are broken*
> *My medicine bags torn*
> *The hair on my loins is singed*
> *The upright post at the gate has fallen* (lines 28–31)

There could be other interpretations of this poem. The idea really is that students will be able to examine more than one side of the coin, where applicable, so that there is more value attached to critical analysis. If it is possible to see more than one side to a poem, the teacher ought to guide the students through the various possibilities so that the poem is not limited to one interpretation. To explain this point further one perhaps needs to refer to Eric S. Ng'maryo's 'I will cling to your garment':

> *I will cling to your garment like a wild grass seed:*
> *I will needle your flesh*
> *And pray*
> *That my insistent call for you*
> *Be not met with*
> *A jerky*
> *Removal*
> *From your garment,*
> *And a throw into the fire,*
> *But that*
> *You will drop me on the fertile ground of*
> *Your favour.* (lines 1–12)

At the literal level, a student who interprets the imagery in this poem as referring to a louse in somebody's garment will be quite right. In this case the louse or even a bug will be seen as seeking protection, warmth and survival by being closer to the human body. But one needs to go deeper than this and see it as a love poem in which the speaker pleads with a woman he loves not to let him down or betray him or mistreat him because of these strong feelings he has for her. He is, in essence, asking her to reciprocate by giving him her hand in marriage.

It would be pointless to attempt to discuss, in this introduction, most of the poems which appear in the anthology. The occasional

15

references have simply been used to illustrate certain points or to focus on certain poetic features with the aim of providing a kind of guide to both the teachers and the students of literature. In this task, as stated before, the special aspects of language must be given due attention so that students can build up a vocabulary within which their expression is apt and confident. We should stress here that a firm background needs to be laid right from Form 1 so that the further the students go the more alert and sensitive to poetry their minds become. They will gradually become aware of the difference between a 'private' poet and a 'public' poet and they will be able to make their own value judgement after having taken a number of factors into consideration. The idea is to develop a critical approach to the study and enjoyment of poetry, whether it is oral or written.

Finally, this anthology does not promise exhaustiveness or conclusiveness with regard to points raised, questions posed or poems chosen. It is merely an addition to the vast literary richness within our cultures and a demonstration of our varied responses to our environments. One hopes that this humble effort will inspire more contributions to the East African literary scene.

A. D. AMATESHE
Kenyatta University (Nairobi)
August 1987

NOTES

[1] Njuguna Mugo, 'Introduction' in Micere Githae Mugo, *Daughter Of My People Sing*, East African Literature Bureau, Nairobi, 1976, p. viii.

[2] Richard Ntiru, *Mawazo*, III, 12 (Dec 1971) p. 60.

[3] Okot p'Bitek, *Horn of My Love*, Heinemann, London, 1974, p. 149.

[4] Isidore Okpewho, *The Heritage of African Poetry*, Longman, London, 1985.

[5] L. S. Senghor, *Prose and Poetry*, Oxford University Press, 1965.

[6] Lennard Okola (ed.), 'Introduction' in *Drum Beat*, East African Publishing House, Nairobi, 1967, p. 13.

[7] Okot p'Bitek, *Africa's Cultural Revolution*, Macmillan, Nairobi, 1973, pp. 22–23.

[8] Ngugi Wa Thiong'o, 'Okot p'Bitek and Writing in East Africa', *Homecoming*, Heinemann, London, 1972.

[9] Jose Tallet, 'Rumba', *African Poetry for Schools; Book 2*, Noel Machin (ed.), Longman, London, 1978, p. 12.

[10] Wole Soyinka, 'The Writer in the African State', *Transition*, 31, (1967), p. 13.

PART ONE

When I see the beauty on my beloved's face

Okot p'Bitek

(An oral love poem among the Acoli community of Northern Uganda)

When I see the beauty on my
    beloved's face,
I throw away the food in my hand;
Oh, sister of the young man, listen;
5 The beauty on my beloved's face.

Her neck is long, when I see it
I cannot sleep one wink;
Oh, the daughter of my mother-in-law,
Her neck is like the shaft of the spear.

10 When I touch the tattoos on her back,
I die;
Oh, sister of the young man, listen;
The tattoos on my beloved's back.

When I see the gap in my beloved's teeth,
15 Her teeth are white like dry season simsim;
Oh, daughter of my father-in-law, listen,
The gap in my beloved's teeth.

The daughter of the bull confuses my head,
I have to marry her;
20 True, sister of the young man, listen;
The suppleness of my beloved's waist.

QUESTIONS

1 What effect does repetition have in this poem?

2 What do you feel the line at the end of every stanza contributes to the poem?

3 What impression do we get from the poem about the speaker's emotions?

4 Why do you think the poet uses an element of exaggeration in this poem?

18

5 From what point of view has the poet composed this piece: from the point of view of his society or from the point of view of the speaker as an individual? Examine the ideas in the poem for your answer.

Beloved of my mother

Okot p'Bitek

(A funeral dirge among the Acoli ethnic group of Northern Uganda)

Beloved of my mother
      is like plucked vegetable leaves;
His large eyes are wide open,
His teeth are white like dry- season
5   simsim;
Death has destroyed a prince,
To- day, he is lost.
Son of the chief,
Beloved of my mother
10 Is like plucked vegetable leaves.

QUESTIONS

1 What is the implication of the title?

2 Identify the images used in the poem. How effective are they?

3 What line in this poem conveys the feeling of emptiness?

4 How has the poet been economical in his expression of emotion here?

A Homecoming

Kalungi Kabuye

I have walked dark streets in my life
      and known the all-enveloping darkness

19

I have sung the rhythmless songs
and danced the drumless beat.

5   I, too, have watched the stars
                I, too, have waited for Him to come
                I, too, have watched love pass me by.

Sitting all alone, the moon frowns on my plight:
                whence shall I go?
10   whither shall I run?
                Where can I hide?

I have lived the prodigal life
                and reached for the silver stars;
I have basked in solitude
15   and felt the pain of loss.

But, I have written out my story with tears and tools of
                                      sorrow
                I have sung out my song on my stringless guitar –
                It dies, and I throw the guitar away.

QUESTIONS

1 How does the poet play on words in lines 3, 4 and 17?

2 Who do you think is being referred to in line 6?

3 Identify any *two* images in the poem. Show that you understand them and comment on their suitability.

4 In your own words, explain what the poet is saying about 'homecoming'.

Destiny

Philippa Namutebi Barlow

Have you ever once felt
as though you were on a road,
a road leading you somewhere
and yet . . . . . nowhere?
5 And at one point or another
felt like jumping off the road

but . . . . . to where?
So you clung onto the road,
pursued it, followed it,
10 because it was all you had;
Because even though your
destination was unknown,
at least you had a destination?
So often these days, I feel like this,
15 and though my destination is
unknown,
I trudge on, wearily, to the end.

QUESTIONS

1 Read the poem carefully. In what way is the title appropriate?

2 How does the poet involve the reader with regard to the subject matter?

3 Identify *one* metaphor in the poem. How effective is it?

4 Why do you think the poet wrote this poem?

Beloved

E. H. S. Barlow

So long as you are there
For the love that we share
I'll take my shield and spear
And life's battle continue without fear
5 When battleweary
Peace will I find always
In your love and quiet ways

Remember our dawn of love
Our struggles and how we grew
10 Through the entangled growth below
That abounds on the dark forest floor
Our vines have reached the light
Behold our golden fruits
True love's gracious gifts divine

So long as we are together
Your hands in mine again
We'll brave life's rough terrain
All set for exciting horizons
After the noon of day
20 We'll travel the sunset way
Behold the glory of a fulfilled day.

QUESTIONS

1 What type of poem would you say this is?

2 Comment on the use of imagery in this poem. (Refer to specific examples).

3 What does this poem tell us about making up one's mind?

4 Write a poem or prose passage describing the kind of life which the man would like to live.

5 Do you think that the poet is serious or is he merely being sentimental?

The Disabled

Bangirana B-T. Kanzira Rwandambwe

Things you've done I'll say
For that way I'll say things
You've not done:
Your charges must never exceed
5 What you paid –
(Any way what did you?)

Beating up the disabled
Is not bravery –
You who received all –
10   You break the crutches of the cripple
    The support of the blind
    You cast over the hedge
    You deafen the blind
    You blind the deaf . . .

15 That way you've done
Egocentricity service.

1 What is the tone of the poem?

2 What is the implication of line 6 in the poem?

3 What makes this poem satirical?

4 What does the poet think of life in his time?

The end begins: words
Kalungi Kabuye

Words words words
words without wind
words without end
without care what action
5   we stand and watch
on fireless fireplaces.

heads of clans stand and stare
they come and go
some die by beheading.
10   clans have no heads
they wait in pain for peace
but peace for scattered skeletons
reeks of bloody emptiness.

down the countryside I know
15   elephants fight daily
but the common grass I know
under their feet
bleeds, starves and dies
under the strain of gunpowder excreted.

20   we are maimed daily
and the mime continues
this time again without words.

QUESTIONS

1 What effect does the repetition of 'words words words . . .' (lines
1–3) have upon the poem?

2 What sort of atmosphere does the poem have? How is this atmosphere created?

3 What images are there in the poem? How do they correspond to the poet's meaning?

4 What is the implication of line 21 within the context of the whole poem?

I will cling to your garment

Eric S. Ng'maryo

I will cling to your garment like a wild grass seed:
I will needle your flesh
And pray
That my insistent call for you
5 Be not met with
A jerky
Removal
From your garment,
And a throw into the fire,
10 But that
You will drop me on the fertile ground of
Your favour.

QUESTIONS

1 In what category can you place this poem?

2 What imagery does the poet employ to communicate his meaning?

3 What sort of atmosphere does the poem have? How is this atmosphere created?

4 Can you draw any general conclusions from this poem?

The Analogy

Bahadur Tejani

Tonight
in the beggar
I saw the whole
of my country.

5   Tied were his hands –
ashamed of use –
for leprosy.

Sunk was his body
– eaten with corruption
10   – of the worm.

Like the
shattered snake
once liquid
now pounded
15   by innumerable feet
he dragged
himself
moisting the pavement
in the process.

20   What may I give?
A bullet in the brain
to end throes
infinitely greater
than death?

25   Or pity?

Is he cheating?

QUESTIONS

Write a critical appreciation of this poem, commenting on the
imagery and anything else that interests you. Say whether you
think the poet makes his point successfully or not, giving reasons
for your opinion.
    Before you start to write, think about:
(a) the title;

(b) the use of leprosy rather than another disease;

(c) the alternative answers to the question 'What may I give?' (line 20);

(d) the last question of all.

Ploughing

Dr Noah K. Ndosi

In the fresh hours
of a labouring day,
two oxen tug a plough,
a whip flying violently
5 in fading echoes
as the farmer's plough
breaks the ground
round after round.
The sun
10 like a chameleon
crawls over high branches
to an overhead hesitation:
the head goes dizzy,
the mouth dries up,
15 hands fumble for snuff.

On a twig,
a piece of cloth
flies in the wind
as exhaustion wells up,
20 the oxen snorting
and one crawling
with tearing defeat.

Solid determination
diluted with pity,
25 the farmer hides the yoke
in nearby bushes;
he frees the beasts
which rejoice
in the last hours
30 of a crushing day;
they feed with greed

before they are escorted
to a cold muddy kraal.

QUESTIONS

1 What impressions are created by the following lines?

  (a) The sun
     like a chameleon
     crawls over high branches
     to an overhead hesitation: (lines 9–12)

  (b) the oxen snorting
     and one crawling
     with tearing defeat. (lines 20–23)

  (c) Solid determination
     diluted with pity, (lines 23–24)

2 Where do you think the poet's sympathies lie? Explain clearly using evidence from the poem.

3 Which lines in the poem tell you that ploughing is an everyday activity for the farmer?

Message bearer

Dr Noah K. Ndosi

Along the way
tip-toed he,
his body light
on the path,
5 as he,
half-runningly walked
invariably changing steps
like a marching soldier,
flinging arms
10 backwards and forwards,
at times sideways,
down and up,
across applauding rivers
of the village

15 bloomed he,
   with the happiness of heart
   as though mounts of agility
   had been restored in him;
   and he entered
20 the adjoining village
   with kingly pride,
   impatient to break the news
   of a new born child.

QUESTIONS

1 How does the poet express his admiration of the message bearer?

2 What techniques does he use for building up the poem towards the climax?

3 What time in history does the poem relate to?

4 Comment on the rhythm of the poem. What contribution does it make to the overall impact of the text?

A fight of roosters

Dr Noah K. Ndosi

In the midst of banana-thickness
sunrays filtered through cowardly,
they fell on a swarm of flies
which buzzingly feasted
5 on fresh cow-droppings
while two cocks
like warriors
viciously fought one another.

Swinging fast pecks of a beak,
10 a rooster hopped high
as it battled the opponent;
apprehension swelled high
and dust like smoke
floated in the air.

28

15 From near homes
little children took sides
cheering up the exciting show;
a cock suffered repeated attacks,
it lost courage and
20 ran away in defeat;
a little spectating child
could not help it;
he shed tears of disappointment.

At some distance away,
25 the fight commenced again;
after moments of strength-testing,
one rolled in a bleeding eye;
the battle stopped mysteriously,
the cocks stared into each other
30 and went apart
as if they had secretly
signed a truce between them.

QUESTIONS

1 How is the overall mood of the poem created by the poet?

2 Can you find any instance(s) of irony in this poem?

.3 Can you draw any general conclusions from this poem?

4 Explain the meaning of the following lines within the context of the poem:
   (a) 'sunrays filtered through cowardly' (line 2).
   (b) 'apprehension swelled high' (line 12).
   (c) 'one rolled in a bleeding eye' (line 27).

The Stubborn One

Dr Noah K. Ndosi

Young and healthy,
he grew up sappy;
he anxiously struck
a long way to distant lands
5 where he ate and drank
as his pockets afforded.

29

From home
filtered many problems
to his distant ears,
10 a strong voice summoned him
to come and bury his own
when death struck at will;
dazzled by the strength
of mid-day of life,
15 he never stirred.

A creeping illness
like a big stick
fell on him:
he weakened,
20 his legs were frail
without touch;
like a helpless child,
he even lost control
of his bowels;
25 in no time
he was rotting sores.

Quite unexpected,
his soul now yearns for repairs;
his stubborn past transformed
30 into an acceptable obligation,
the God, who never existed
despite tolling Sunday-bells
is now ever present
his eyes soaked
35 in painful tears,
his tongue often melts
in soft sessions of prayers:
if only he would get well,
he would . . . . .

QUESTIONS

1 *Allusion* is one of the techniques in literary writing. From your
own knowledge, state in what way this is applicable to this
poem.

2 Find examples of the poet's use of similes. How effective are
they?

3 What other title might you suggest for this poem? Why?

4 What is your reaction to the kind of situation the poet is describing in the poem?

Illegal Brew

Dr Noah K. Ndosi

He was a man
of favoured health,
whose speech was clarity
– a successful player
5 in the mysterious game
of fluctuating life

The beginning
was only a few sips;
but each time,
10 he hit the fullness
of bulging calabashes

Time pulled on;
his head entered a pot
and remained
15 firmly stuck in;
his head flooding
with intoxicating
currents of alcohol,
he is now the last
20 to leave the beer markets.

Despite floods of warnings
from families and friends,
he firmly transplanted
his young life
25 on the lip-burning
illegal brew

Of late,
his bowels have become
visibly distended;
30 his breath short

and shallow,
he also drags thickly
swollen limbs.

Beyond despair,
35 he sees the leveller coming
to add him to a list
like some heedless neighbour
who perished the same way.

QUESTIONS

1 What meaning do you get from the first stanza?

2 What contrast does this meaning make to the rest of the poem?

3 Which expressions used in this poem are striking to you? In what ways?

4 What do you understand by 'leveller' (line 35) within the context of the poem?

5 What is this poem really about, in terms of everyday life?

After the rains

Dr Noah K. Ndosi

After the thirsty earth
has sucked in water,
soft darkness of rich soil
attracts the wandering eye.

5 The grass along paths
shoots to the waist,
as they eagerly nibble
at fresh tips,
goats uplift their heads;
10 sheep do not bend low
for bulky browsing;
over splashes of droppings,
little flies dance vigorously.

The sun glides gracefully
15 over the land,
green fertility

32

dances before the eye,
the wind bends
young shoots gently
20 and birds fill the air
with many delightful tunes.

Little children imitate
beasts of the wilderness;
they play hide and seek
25 and blood fills up to brims;
then,
heavy pours of rain
have once again
sparked deep life
30 into titillating rhythm.

The spirit of thankfulness
evokes deep belief
in an omnipotent hand,
from whose secret heights
35 sweet life vibrates,
hope and certainty
like full moon
leading mankind on and on.

QUESTIONS

1 What type of poem would you say this is?

2 How does the poet develop the theme of the poem? Use specific
illustrations from the text.

3 How would you interpret the last stanza of the poem?

Song of the Worker

E. Songoyi

We squat
We move
Left centre right
Breaking stones
5 Kwa! Kwa! Kwa!

Our hands sore
Our heads ache
Our knees numb
Our backs break
10 Breaking stones
Kwa! Kwa! Kwa!

We squat
We move
Back centre forward
15 Tilling the land
Kwa! Kwa! Kwa!

Our song is sorrow
Our tears we eat
In rags we move
20 Tramping the land
Kwa! Kwa! Kwa!
To them:
It's dance
They roar in laughter
25 While we sweat and bleed

To them:
It's pleasure
They weep with laughter
While we stumble and tumble
30 Burdened and hungry
Kwa! Kwa! Kwa! Kwa! Kwa!

QUESTIONS

1 Find the words or lines which create the mood of the poem.

2 How does the poet use *onomatopoeia* to help us understand the subject of the poem?

3 If you were to perform this poem, what would you do to dramatise its meaning?

4 How does the poet use contrast to present his ideas in the poem?

Turn-boy

Richard S. Mabala

The bus squealed sluggishly to a halt
Before the bulging kanzu'd form
Of an immaculately dressed old man
Beside five jutting sacks of coconuts.

5   Even before the halt
Out sprang the turn-boy
Young
Ragged
Shirt fraying before the muscles on his arm.

10 Shikamoo Baba –
Marahaba;
And without another word
He tossed the first sack
Onto his mighty shoulders
15 And raced to toss it once more
Onto the roof of the bus.

Meanwhile
The watchful gaze of the kanzu
Never wavered
20 And we in the bus
Only grumbled at the delay.
The second and third sacks
Quickly followed
The fourth, a struggle
25 And the fifth . . . my friend
Gone was the spring
No longer did he toss
Sweat and dust streaked the ragged shirt
And straining muscles beneath
30 Knees faltered as the fifth sack
Was slowly heaved to his shoulders
And when he reached the ladder
And began the arduous climb
It seemed unending,
35 Knees shaking uncontrollably
Beneath the accumulated strain
Shoulders sagging
Mouth twisted
In a grimace of pain

40 And fear of failure
We watched . . .
And held our breath . . .
As the offending sack
Perched precariously on
45 Shaking shoulders
Teetered on the edge.
Below,
The Kanzu's gaze never wavered.
Only the eyes knotted
50 In concern
For his coconuts
Threatened by this weakling of a turn-boy.

And inside,
While we gazed
55 And sighed in relief
When finally the offending load
Landed
With a thump
On the roof above our heads
60 We complained
And grumbled at the delay.

But one man cried out
Jamani!
That young man
65 So strong and lithe
Can only do this work for six months

Any longer
And his neck will be bent,
Permanently
70 Like a bow.
We wanted to laugh
And turned to ridicule this man of pity
Work is work
How else can the loads be lifted?
75 But when we turned to face the speaker
We found a man not so young,
Huge muscles decaying
Evidence of former strength
But his neck . . .
80 Bent like a bow.

Our mocking words stuck in our throats!

QUESTIONS

1 Is the poem serious, or is it comic?

2 What impression of the 'kanzu'd form' (line 2) does the poet create in the poem?

3 Pick out all the words or images in the poem which produce suspense.

4 What do you think are the poet's feelings towards the turn-boy?

5 Find examples of the poet's use of dialogue in this poem. What effect does it have?

6 What do you think of this poem? Give reasons for your answer.

Where are those songs?

Micere Githae Mugo

Where are those songs
my mother and yours
always sang
fitting rhythms
5 to the whole
vast span of life?

What was it again
they sang
     harvesting maize, threshing millet, storing the
10   grain . . .

What did they sing
bathing us, rocking us to sleep . . .
and the one they sang
stirring the pot
15 (swallowed in parts by choking smoke)?

What was it
the woods echoed
as in long file
my mother and yours and all the women on our ridge
20 beat out the rhythms
trudging gaily
as they carried
piles of wood

37

through those forests
25 miles from home
What song was it?

And the row of bending women
hoeing our fields
to what beat
30 did they
break the stubborn ground
as they weeded
our *shambas*?

What did they sing
35 at the ceremonies
       child-birth
       child-naming
       second birth
       initiation . . .?
40 how did they trill the *ngemi*
What was
the warriors' song?
how did the wedding song go?
sing me
45 the funeral song.
What do you remember?

Sing
       I have forgotten
       my mother's song
50   my children
       will never know.
This I remember:
Mother always said
       sing child sing
55   make a song
       and sing
       beat out your own rhythms
       the rhythms of your life
       but make the song soulful
60   and make life
       sing

Sing daughter sing
around you are
uncountable tunes
65 some sung
others unsung

sing them
to your rhythms
observe
70 listen
absorb
soak yourself
bathe
in the stream of life
75   and then sing
         sing
         simple songs
         for the people
         for all to hear
80   and learn
         and sing
         with you

QUESTIONS

1 Read the poem very carefully. What categories of songs is the poet referring to?

2 What is her intention? (Refer to the poem as closely as possible).

3 Comment on the technical devices in the poem.

4 What is the implication of the following lines?
   (a) I have forgotten
       my mother's song
       my children
       will never know.   (lines 48–51)

   (b) beat out your own rhythms
       but make the song soulful   (lines 57–59)

Despair

Edwin Waiyaki

I have heard the leaves fall
From the trees with the soft patter
Of rats' feet on bare board.

39

The tiring mourners,
5 Lift gaunt hands skywards
In sad supplication.

They pray,
The stripped skeletons pray
To the season-god to return their summer.

10   And the god gives his answer
     Of the hissing wind,
     Chilling to the bone

Oh I have heard the leaves fall
From the trees like the soft tread
15 Of my beloved's sandals on bare boards.

And I,
Lone watcher in the woods
Lost in the midst of evening twilight
Turn misted eyes to heaven
20 And I pray
To Him of autumn and of the howling wind:
I pray,
I stripped skeleton pray
Would she could wake –
25 Still, ashen figure in long robe of white;
I pray,
I stooped skeleton pray
Would she could rise,
Serene stricken figure in long robe of white.

30   But God gives his answer
     In the scourging wind . . . .
     Stinging to the bone.

QUESTIONS

1 Comment on the tone of the poem.

2 What effect do you think the poet is trying to produce by the use of repetition?

3 Explain the relationship between line 19 and the title of the poem.

4 Discuss the expressions here which most vividly reveal the speaker's desperation.

5 Comment on the effectiveness of the last three lines of this poem.

6 What would you say about the stanza pattern and in what way(s) does it contribute to the overall impact of the poem?

Their City

Lennard Okola

City in the sun
without any warmth
except for *wanaotosheka**
and the tourists escaping
5 from civilized boredom

Sit under the Tree
any Saturday morning
and watch the new Africans,
the anxious faces
10 behind the steering wheels
in hire purchase cars,
see them looking important
in a tiny corner
behind the chaüffeur

15 We have seen them
in a nightmare,
the thickset directors
of several companies;
we have seen them
20 struggling under the weight
of a heavy lunch
on a Monday afternoon
cutting a tape

to open a building,
25 we have seen them
looking over their
gold-rimmed glasses
to read a speech
And in the small hours
30 between one day and the next
we have strolled through
the deserted streets
and seen strange figures
under bougainvillea bushes

41

35 in traffic islands,
    figures hardly human
    snoring away into
    the cold winds of the night;
    desperately dying to live.

wanaotosheka – Swahili word for those who are satisfied –
    symbolically, those who are privileged.

QUESTIONS

1 Who are the 'we' in the poem?

2 How does the poet portray 'the new Africans' mentioned in line 8?

3 What contribution does the satire the poet uses make to the meaning of the poem?

4 What is implied by the following lines?
   (a) 'gold-rimmed glasses' (line 27)

   (b) 'the deserted streets' (line 32)

   (c) 'figures hardly human
        desperately dying to live.' (lines 36–39)

Extensions

Humphrey Webuye

    When I did marry you
    I married not your clan
    And it was never my plan

    Now I remain encumbered
5   With a blanket for grandparents
    Money for your parents
    And presents for your siblings

    Today it is your uncle
    Tomorrow comes your aunt
10 The next day is your aunt's
    cousin's younger daughter

Then your brother's younger
wife's cousin from Misango.

The whole clan comes
15 Expecting me to keep smiling
Expecting me to keep giving
Expecting me to keep loving
When I should be worrying
When I should be lamenting
20 At how slow our people
Are at adapting to
Modernity and development.
Why are gerontologists
Taking long to come for
25 Those wrinkled old bones?
Why can't people learn
That we need privacy?

Why the extended greetings
Extended begging hands
30 Extended vexing expectations
Extended immense families
Extended systems of egalitarianism
Extended marriage extensions
With redistributive mechanisms?

35 Why can't people learn
That we need privacy?
Why have they done this to me?
Why have they?
Why?

QUESTIONS

1 Find a dictionary and look up the hard words in the poem. Are
you now able to interpret the basic issues in the poem?

2 Pick out the expressions which especially give a feeling of
uneasiness.

3 What kind of relationship do you think exists between the
speaker and the one being addressed?

4 Put what the poem says into your own words. Do you agree or
disagree with what it says? Why?

Come, My Mother's Son

Lillian Ingonga

Come, my mother's son
You're no longer a baby
Stop following the women
To the firesides
5 Stop peeping in the cooking pot
Stop pinching the girls
You're no longer a baby
You are a man

Come, my mother's son
10 Show your bravery
And step fully into manhood
The test is not hard
Not with determination

Let not the women chirp
15 And giggle in mockery
And call you names
Come, my mother's son
Show and prove your bravery
And rightfully claim your stand
20 Among the young warriors

My mother's son,
Shine your prowess
As a great warrior, a dancer
A great player, a sprinter
25 And get yourself admirers
Get a bride of your choice
Come, my mother's son
Let's see your test

Come, my mother's son
30 Heed to prove your manhood
Cultivate the trees of your forefathers
For a continual bloom and fruit bearing
Carry on your father's name into the future
Come, my mother's son
35 Cower not, stand as a man
And let us see you are a man

1 With what effect does the poet manipulate punctuation?

2 What oral devices can you identify in the poem?

3 How does the poet portray the nature of her society and what is her intention?

4 Do you find the poem appealing? If so, why?

Betrothed

Obyero Odhiambo

The bride, they said
had gone through school
primary secondary university upwards:
Three thousand shillings is not enough.

5 For having fed her
              schooled her
              employed her
Three thousand shillings is not enough –

For having borne her
10   cared her
              doctored her
And 'she is pure'
Three thousand shillings is not enough.

Look at her silky black hair
15 Darker and finer than that
Flywhisk there
Look at her forehead, a
Nice wide trace between
hairline and eyes:
20 'She is immensely intelligent.'

Look at her eyes. Yes, look again
Two diviners' cowries spread out
symbolically on the divination mat
deep profound intelligent;
25 Look at those lips 'ndugu' . . .
Three thousand shillings is not enough
even to shake her by the hand.

'Fathers, this is what we walked with!
Three thousand shillings
30 As a token of our
Love
for your daughter and you
our intended kin
It was just a token
35 The size of the token does not reflect
The size of the heart that bringeth it
My heart is full to the brim with
Love
for your daughter
40 Mine is just a token of my
Love
for her and you my intended kin.'

But, young man, you say, you love
and you possibly expect love
45 But, young man, don't you
Don't you really feel
Three thousand shillings is not enough
even to get love?
Three thousand shillings is not enough!

QUESTIONS

1 Critically comment on the technical devices in the poem.

2 What do you think of this poem? Give reasons for your answer.

3 Do you think there is any deeper meaning in this poem or is it a straightforward piece of description?

Witness

Obyero Odhiambo

I witnessed yet again today
Something I wish I'd not say –
The lowering of a loved one
Into earth's deep belly
5 The deep dark grave like a cave.

The father sighed: tears long dry
The mother moaned: voice now hoarse
The grandfather swore to take
Deputation to him above
10 Brothers with soily hands, rubbed
Their ashen faces, sombre looks
Their tired eyes sinking deeper in their sockets
An aunt wrung out a shrill wail
For days unending refusing to be comforted –

15 Lower and lower it went
its sweet-nut yellow violently clashing with
the mean brownblack of the depths
It rested at the bottom of the pit
His spirits rock bottom:
20 Never shall we again re-witness
though many more we'll see
Into
The deep dark grave like a cave.

QUESTIONS

1 Illustrate from any part of the poem how the poet's choice of
words helps to create the mood of the poem.

2 What do the words 'His spirits rock bottom' (line 19) contribute
to the meaning of the whole poem?

3 What other title might you suggest for this poem? Why?

4 What is the implication of the last stanza?

Wedding eve

Dr Everett Standa

Should I
Or should I not
Take the oath to love
For ever
5 This person I know little about?

Does she love me
Or my car
Or my future
Which I know little about?

10 Will she continue to love me
When the future she saw in me
Crumbles and fades into nothing
Leaving the naked me
To love without hope?

15 Will that smile she wears
Last through the hazards to come
When fate strikes
Across the dreams of tomorrow?

Or will she,
20 Like the clever passenger in a faulty plane,
Wear her life jacket
And jump out to save her life
Leaving me to crash into the unknown?

What magic can I use
25 To see what lies beneath
Her angel face and well knit hair
To see her hopes and dreams
Before I take the oath
To love forever?

30 We are both wise chess players
She makes a move
I make a move
And we trap each other in our secret dreams
Hoping to win against each other.

QUESTIONS

1 At about what time do you think this poem was written? Why?

2 What effect does the use of rhetoric have within the poem?

3 The poet is trying to say something about the bride. Explain what this is in your own words.

4 What does the poem generally tell you about marriage?

The Moslem Grave-Digger

Jared Angira

Brother
        it is wet this morning
        which seems a relief for you
        the graveyard is soft

5 you are digging
into the cold chest
of the earth
into sleepless bones
of the dead

10 Brother
        in the understanding
        we believe in the resurrection
        of the dead
        which you seem to discount
15   on the basis of daily bread
tears
        mingle with rainwater
        and flow

from the old graves
20 what explanation
what defence
        will you mount
        when on the ideal day
        (not for lawyers)
25   When on revelation day
        all skeletons come trudging by
        seeking explanations
        and supplementary informations
to this persistent disturbance by your blood drenched
                        hoe?

QUESTIONS

1 Why do you think the emphasis of the poet should be on the 'Moslem' grave-digger?

2 Identify the words which create the mood of this poem.

3 Comment on the use of imagery in the poem.

4 What does this poem say about human values?

5 What does line 24 imply within the context of the last stanza?

Braying on and on . . .

Jared Angira

It is now years
since
I stood
in this cold bitterness
5 jailed in this
      unperfumed garden

It is many years
of fruitless howls
from this cell
10 under the deeps

Imprisoned
in this dark cocoon
in sarcasm
      deranged
15 in dishonour
      defiled
in agony
      tortured
in male degradation
20   raped
hands in sisal ropes behind my back
free legs, free mouth, where can I walk and talk?

It is fairly long
from the undertaking
25 the hot methylated spirit
sprinkled over the red wound
but the bitterness of the methylated spirit
lasts only a few seconds
Yet it is really long, long
30   since I started
If there is no outlet, perhaps there will be one
      when organs are cold.

50

1 Read the poem very carefully. What do you now think is the significance of the title?

2 What words are repeated in the poem and what effect do they have on the subject matter?

3 Discuss the condition of the speaker as indicated in the poem.

4 What interpretation do you give to the last two lines of the poem?

At your feet

Musaemura Bonas Zimunya

We die
all tears and blood
pain and grief and ghosts,
Mighty One,

5 We the poor
the dispossessed
the peaceless
the fear-smitten
unfreed slaves,

10 We die at your feet.

QUESTIONS

1 What type of poem would you say this is?

2 What is the significance of the title?

3 What is the poet's intention in this poem?

4 What words in the poem show the speaker's emotions?

An African Thunderstorm

David Rubadiri

From the west
Clouds come hurrying with the wind
Turning sharply
Here and there
5   Like a plague of locusts
Whirling,
Tossing up things on its tail
Like a madman chasing nothing.

Pregnant clouds
10 Ride stately on its back,
Gathering to perch on hills
Like dark sinister wings;
The wind whistles by
And trees bend to let it pass.

15 In the village
Screams of delighted children
Toss and turn
In the din of the whirling wind;
Women –
20 Babies clinging on their backs –
Dart about
In and out
Madly;
The wind whistles by
25 Whilst trees bend to let it pass.

Clothes wave like tattered flags
Flying off
To expose dangling breasts
As jagged blinding flashes
30 Rumble, tremble, and crack
Amidst the smell of fired smoke
And the pelting march of the storm.

QUESTIONS

1 What sort of atmosphere does the poem have?
How is this atmosphere created?

2 What is the deeper meaning of the following lines:

(a) From the west
Clouds come hurrying with the wind (lines 1–2)

(b) Pregnant clouds
Ride stately on its back (lines 9–10)

(c) The wind whistles by
And trees bend to let it pass (lines 13–14)

(d) Clothes wave like tattered flags
Flying off
To expose dangling breasts (lines 26–28)

3 What else in the poem is suggested through the poet's choice of words?

Yet Another Song

David Rubadiri

Yet another song
I have to sing:
In the early wake
Of a colonial dusk
5   I sang the song of fire.

The church doors opened
To the clang
Of new anthems
And colourful banners.

10   Like the Beatles,
The evangelical hymns
Of conversion
Rocked the world and me.

I knelt before the new totems
15   I had helped to raise,
Watered them
With tears of ecstasy.

They grew
Taller than life,
20   Grimacing and breathing fire.

Today
I sing yet another song,
A song of exile.

QUESTIONS

1 What do you think has happened to give rise to the poem?

2 How do the speaker's feelings change during the poem?

3 What is the deeper meaning of the fourth stanza?

4 How does the poet use rhythm to help us appreciate the poem?

PART TWO

Serenade

Philippa Namutebi Barlow

Sing me a serenade,
a serenade about you.
Through your music talk to me,
let me understand you more.
5 Tell me about your pain,
about your sorrow.
Tell me about your happiness
and let me follow.
Let me see you as you are,
10 not as the world thinks you are.
I do not want to understand
what you show the world.
I want to know that real you,
that you in your song,
15 that innermost you that
you share with your song.
I want to understand you,
to understand your song.
Please, sing me the serenade,
20 the serenade of your life,
and maybe someday it might mingle,
might mingle with mine,
that our serenades together
might become as one.

QUESTIONS

1 What is a serenade?

2 Does this poem have a lyrical quality? Support your answer with examples.

3 Consider all the ways in which the poet conveys her feelings towards the subject of the poem.

4 What are her expectations? Refer to specific lines within the poem.

Second burial

Ejiet Komolo

When thunder rolls in the wilderness
Like a drum
The time has come
To perform the second burial of your departed
5 You never saw their graves
But you shall kill the sacrificial ram
Over the memories
Which caress the anthill of your bosom
Like the bull of a herd,

10 Remove the mound of vigil ashes
From your compound
And bury it with your sackcloth
Rip the headband of your wife's sorrow
Tip warm water into your palm
15 And rinse your salty face

Because when your womenfolk
Go to the well for the first time tomorrow
It is time to swallow your sorrow
And erect a new homestead.

QUESTIONS

1 What is the tone of the poem?

2 Who is the poet addressing?

3 What is the cultural significance of the poem?

4 Comment on the technical devices in the poem, paying particular
attention to the choice of words.

Horizons

Kalungi Kabuye

as I meditate
and levitate

in a human state
no one can see
5 how the internal sea
wells up with hope
but let's hope
life so dear
with love so near
10 and closeness so close
will bring home
to all at home
the thing that we hope
means to transform
15 even the simplest digit
into a magnified seed
of a mustard tree.

QUESTIONS

1 Comment on the rhythm, rhyme and anything else that you notice in this poem.

2 What else in the poem is *suggested* through the poet's choice of words?

3 What interpretation do you give to the title of the poem?

The Deep Freezer

Richard S. Mabala

Status reminder of the study tour
It grunted quietly in the corner
Admired by all
But unopened
5 For it was empty.

One day
Her only child
Triumphant inspiration in game of hide and seek
Heaved open the lid
10 Dived into flaking rust

And shut out the light
For ever

The freezer had won its first meat.

QUESTION

Write a critical appreciation of this poem, commenting on the imagery. Say whether you think the poet makes his point successfully or not, giving reasons for your opinion.

Vicious Circle

Makando E. A. Mandia

Master Fisherman
Drops the hook
Concealed in tasty flesh

Hungry,
5 I swallowed it whole
Rotting flesh of my brother

Comrades,
Beware my fate!
Stretched beneath the scorching sun
10 New bait to hide that hook
Which lurks for you.

QUESTIONS

1 What do you understand by the title of this poem?

2 Is there any element of personification in the poem? If so, how effective is it?

3 What is the significance of line 6 in the context of the whole poem?

4 What do you think is the deeper meaning of the poem?

The Bored Wife

Freddy Macha

a hand and a loose one at that
hangs
drearily
lazily
5 at the door's mouth

eyes
loll about as if disliking sleep
hating to keep awake

she stays at the door
10 every hour of the morning
every hour of the day and night
but mostly in the morning
watching the people passing by

a snake of jealousy crosses her thick lips
15 as she watches lip-sticked, powdered women
with leather and plastic handbags
also going to work
also coming from work

her hand
20 pushes the rusty door
to and fro; to and fro
the old hinges of the tired metal
seem to wail
and weep
25 quietly

there she is
each morning at the half-opened door
her back turned against 'trouble-some' kids
and the shop-keeping husband
30 busy counting money
inside the big house . . .

QUESTIONS

1 This is a depressing poem. Pick on specific words or expressions
to illustrate this.

2 What do you think is the *setting* of this poem?

3 What impression do you get about the society within which the poem is set?

4 Which expressions in the poem suggest the passing of time?

5 What else in the poem is not made explicit but is *suggested* through the poet's choice of words?

Back Home

Jwani Mwaikusa

And one day I went back home:
Back to the old homestead
With a ring of old huts
Surrounding a wide compound
5 Swept clean for children to play
And yell and laugh and cry.
I walked briskly, thinking of home:
Smoke rising from the huts
Filtered through the thatched roofs
10 Dripping wet after a shower of rain;
Moist ground in the compound,
Grandpa sitting on his stool
And sipping from his gourd;
Birds singing in the mango tree.

15 And then, finally, I reached home:
The air heavy with silence
Huts, down in dry heaps of dilapidation
Shoots of scorched elephant grass
Growing piously in the compound;
20 A carpet of mango leaves
Falling on the mound of earth
Under which was buried but the tip –
Yes, only the tip of grandpa's walking staff
Could be seen peeping from under the earth
25 Pointing down to where the owner lay:
The lasting indication
Of his inability to talk again
Except by echoes of silence
Telling me I went back too late.

1 Identify the expressions which create the mood of this poem.

2 Which other expressions used in this poem are striking to you? In what ways?

3 How effectively has the poet used the setting of the poem to portray change? (Describe the change itself).

4 What feelings does the poet show for this change? Use the evidence from the text to illustrate your answer.

A Writer's Poem

Innocent Karamagi

I want to write a poem
a poem with a message
embellished with
images
5 symbols
subtle allusions
which even critics and poets
let aside other readers
will read and re-read
10 teasing their brains with wonder and thought
giving learned interpretations
in search of my 'original' meaning.

I want to write that poem
but
15 should I?

QUESTIONS

1 What is the tone of the poem?

2 Comment on the effectiveness of the punctuation the poet uses.

3 What impression of the speaker do you get from the poem?

4 In what ways does this poem give you a basic definition and indicate the scope of poetry?

Facelift For Kafira

Francis Imbuga

Though you belong here still
You've lost something of that purity
That brought tears of joy
To my saddened eyes.

5 Your smile is no longer
The first cockcrow of each passing day
And your walk is the walk
Of a tired traveller

Yet I blame you not
10 My innocent one.
You were a mere rabbit
Trapped in the vices of the mighty.

Each time you stood before me
And smiled a million years of hope
15 I knew I would take it all,
A challenge well cherished.

And now is my turn, Kafira, my turn
It is I that will rekindle
that fire that burned gently
20 Beneath your maiden name

With a heart full of the warm
Blood of a long deprived groom
I know I will take it all
For it is a challenge well cherished.

25 With luke-warm water and soft cotton fingers
I will wash you gently each passing day
Yes, I will rid you of that foreign smell
And render it forever, a thing of the past.

Then tomorrow they will come and say,
30 Look, what tears of joy!
What purity!
What warmth, KAFIRA!

As you shine brightly to crown
A challenge well cherished.

1 What is the implication of the title?

2 Who do you imagine is speaking these lines?

3 Is it a cheerful or depressing poem? Give reasons.

4 What feelings does the poet show for Kafira? How does he communicate them?

5 Find examples of the poet's use of imagery and repetition in this poem. What effect do they have?

6 Does this poem have a lyrical quality? Explain.

7 What else in the poem is not made explicit but is *suggested* through the poet's choice of words?

Drowned in the Murmuring Crowd

A. D. Amateshe

When the whisk flies
in mid-air exclamation,
my teeth become one
with those of the crowd;
5 when they smile their nothings
my cheeks wrinkle.

Why do I laugh
in measurements of sweat
my lips cracking
10 with the stress of a slogan?

I am lost in the fidgeting crowd
stretching out my shortness
to have at least a glimpse
of the retreating convoy . . .

15 Yet I prolong my laughter
drowned in the murmuring crowd
on my journey home:

Why did I laugh
when I should have been silent
20 listening to the promises?

QUESTIONS

1 What is the general mood of the poem?

2 In what category can you place this poem?

3 Comment on the poet's use of irony.

4 Although this poem records the experience of an individual, does
it in any way have significance for everyone?

5 How do the questions in stanza two and stanza five contribute to
the effectiveness of this poem?

6 What is the symbolic meaning of stanza 3?

At A Zebra Crossing

A. D. Amateshe

Pedestrians crush into each other
(not with any intended harm)
and curse bitterly as they rush
to either side of the road:

5 It is the evening crucial hour
when each one of them
hurries to secure a place
for the unpredictable night.

Suddenly, within the grace period,
10 a woman holds up her child
against a sightless Kenya bus
in an attempt to live another day –

two generations smashed in an instant:
the bus driver took off
15 to escape the wrath of tramps;
he clung desperately to his single life

While along the Zebra Crossing
lay mother against child
in steaming mixture of red and white
20 awaiting the next of kin.

The police and the ambulance
arrived in speedy procession
to take details of those
who would never ever hear the case!

25 But duty had been done
certified in black and white;
the on-lookers had no more to watch
save the clock-tower which stood in silence.

QUESTIONS

1 What is this poem really about, in terms of everyday life?

2 What does the poet mean when he says, 'within the grace
period?' (line 9)

3 What impression do you get from the poem about the on-lookers?

4 What is the significance of the last line of the poem?

5 What do you think was the poet's intention in writing this poem?

Nyalgunga*

A. D. Amateshe

Come, come!

Son of the Lowland
we are taking you home
back to your ancestral soils.

5 Come with us, our son!

a big welcome awaits you:
magenga*, the big fire, will be lit
to keep away the cold of the Athi Plains.

Don't be afraid, our son,

10 tero buru* will be performed

66

to destroy the demons
that will have followed you –

the occasion is set, our son,

sleepless nights for *nyatiti** players
15 and dancers making formations
behind your symbol of boybood;

So come and join us:

A man you are now
timely returning home
20 from strangeland, a wanderer –

Clad in a lawyer's wig and gown
you have fought battles,
battles with violent criminals,
battles with social injustice.

25 You led a selfless life –

Now, you return home, a hero,
crowned in a silent casket
your speech and sight embalmed.

You will need a guide, our son,

30 for you to reach the *chiel*
which protects Oyugi's homestead
in the crosswind of Nyamila;

You will need an interpreter, our son,

for you to understand the *bul*
35 and its steady, solemn rhythm
correspond to the revving motor-cade.

Do not retreat then, our brother,

when you hear the stampede,
even from your mysterious distance,
40 of a people singing your praises.

Traditional law or written law?

What judgement shall we pass
On those who abandoned us
When they wandered into the unknown?

45 The ancestors still sit, waiting –

magenga, tero buru, nyatiti:

were these museum terms in your life?
Were they not the bloodline of your people?

But come, our brother!
50 Son of Nyalgunga, why the fear?
the elders are beckoning you –
know you not? A man's home is at home.

*Nyalgunga (title): Name of a prominent village in Siaya District,
               Nyanza Province, western Kenya;
magenga   (line 7): among the Luo community of western Kenya,
               the big fire which is usually lit during a funeral,
tero buru   (line 10): a traditional ceremony involving bulls and men
               in war-gear, performed in honour of the dead
               (depending on age and social standing) and also as a
               means of chasing away evil spirits;
nyatiti   (line 14): a traditional musical instrument used by
               recognized traditional composers and singers among the
               Luo community;
chiel   (line 30): traditional fence around a homestead;
bul   (line 34): a traditional, symbolic drum.

QUESTIONS

1 Discuss the shifts of mood in this poem.

2 Comment on the oral devices in the poem. What effect does the
poet achieve by employing them?

3 What do you think is the central theme in the poem?

4 One basic problem in the thematic classification of poetry is that a
poem may have certain elements which qualify it to be classified
as much under one theme as another. What other theme(s) might
this poem come under?

5 Identify and discuss the words or expressions in this poem that
represent separation from traditional culture.

6 Explain the full meaning of the following lines:
   (a) 'and dancers making formations
      behind your symbol of boyhood' (lines 15–16)

   (b) 'your speech and sight embalmed' (line 28)

   (c) 'when you hear the stampede,
      even from your mysterious distance' (lines 38–39)

   (d) 'Were they not the bloodline of your people?' (line 48).

A Johannesburg Miner's Song

Geoffrey K. King'ei

To toil and soil
In the earth's bowels
To reconcile Nature and Man.
Work cannot break me
5   Nor labour enslave me.
Nothing to slacken, dampen my spirit –
My stony will.

I have a will to march on
A common destiny to reach
10   To harmonise history and nature
To reclaim, restore my forgotten individuality
And brotherhood long denied and abused.

I must march on
Brother or foe
15   History and nature must triumph
For I have a stony will.

I will mime and mime
My call to all
Brother and foe
20   My song is for the future
For the future
We all must now sing.

QUESTIONS

1 Identify two instances of *assonance*. What effect do they have?

2 What does the poet mean by lines 3 and 10?

3 What do you understand by the reference to 'my forgotten individuality' in line 11?

4 What impression do you get about the Johannesburg miner with regard to his social vision?

Let Us Talk Together

Dr Everett Standa

Come
Let us talk together
Forget your theories and factories,
Let us talk about ourselves;
5 You and me.

Have you wondered why
We fear each other as we do?
Why you worry about my colour
And not my inside?
10 Why, like a bull in the arena,
You charge at me without thinking,

Have you wondered why
Even after all your education
In psychology and sociology
15 In logic and biology
In mathematics and the bible
You still can't think
Without reacting at my skin colour?

Do not tell me about history
20 For you and me were not born when it happened
Have you wondered why
You call me a criminal in Southern Africa
And unqualified elsewhere in the world?

And now I hear
25 You want to build a bridge
On which you can cross your culture
Into my culture
In what you call
Cross-culture communication.

30 My friend,
Is culture the cause of our fear
Of ourselves?
Have you wondered why?

I still bleed and hurt
35 From the wounds of our hatred
Of each other,
Here I stand facing you.

1 Who do you think the speaker is addressing?

2 What contradictions does the poem bring out?

3 Have you noticed anything about Standa's poetic technique that pleases you as you read the poem?

4 How would you interpret the last line of the poem?

A Pregnant School Girl

Dr Everett Standa

He paid for her seat in the matatu
And walked away;
As he disappeared in the city crowd
All her dreams vanished;

5 One more passenger squeezed in
And lit a cigarette,
She opened the window
And spat cold saliva out,
As the cigarette smoke intensified
10 She wanted to vomit:

She remembered the warm nights
When she was her man's pet,
She remembered the promises
The gifts, the parties, the dances –

15 She remembered her classmates at school
Who envied her expensive shoes,
Lipstick, wrist watch, handbag
Which she brought to school
After a weekend with him

20 The future stood against her
Dark like a night without the moon,
And silent like the end of the world;

As the matatu sped away from the city
She began to tremble with fear
25 Wondering what her parents would say;

With all hope gone
She felt like a corpse
going home to be buried.

QUESTIONS

1 Who is being referred to in the first three lines of the poem?

2 Relate the fifth stanza to the rest of the poem. How effective is the imagery used?

3 Comment on the use of contrast in the poem.

4 How appropriate are the last two lines of the poem?

Conversation on African names

Dr Everett Standa

My dear
I've been thinking
That we should name the baby –
like it used to be in our grandpa's time –
5 after somebody in our ethnic line, you know,
Because the child must have some identity
And not just Patrick Johnson,
David Stewberry, Peter Maclizzard, Charles Shoemaker,
Kim Peking, Kennedy Dickson . . .

10 You see
I know you value these English
Or, Christian names as they are often called,
but we do not want to lose our identity
like that!
15 God will not refuse you just because
you are called Ochieng Adala, or Wekesa Makesi,
or Wanjiko Kimani, or whatever other;
Or, let us put it this way,
Supposing you were born, say
20 One thousand years in the future,

72

And you went to the future museum
And picked a book
Written by some fellow by the name
'Bogus Crankshaft'
25 And, on reading, you discovered later
that this was a real name of a famous
African philosopher, engineer, or whatever;
Wouldn't you wish
The man were called Mutali or Okello
30 Instead of some meaningless so-called Christian names
Bogus Crankshaft!

QUESTIONS

1 Is the poem serious, or is it comic?

2 Can you explain what the poet is saying about African names?

3 What significance does the name 'Bogus Crankshaft' (lines 24 and 31) have in the context of the poem?

4 What is your reaction to the type of conflict which the poet describes in the poem?

Important Things First, Dearest

Arthur Luvai

When the phone rang
My breath
I had just taken and held
Sitting bare-arsed
5 in the small room.

Panic Pants-down – panic
Such a painful decision
Dearest
Your sweet voice and promise of . . . . .
10 Or . . . . .?
I let go my breath and all
Such a relief

To the rumble of the flush of
Clearing and forwarding
15 Downstairs I rushed
To grab the phone.

Then you hang up
Dearest
Stupidly
20 I wrote these lines
Which I must tear up now
After all it might have been
"Wrong number"
Dearest.

QUESTIONS

1 Read the poem carefully and comment on whether or not the title is appropriate.

2 What is the effect of line 2 and line 3 on the tone of the poem?

3 What effect does the repetition of the word 'panic' in line 6 have upon the poem?

4 Have you noticed anything about Luvai's poetic technique that pleases you as you read the poem?

The Death of My Father

Dr Henry Indangasi

His sunken cheeks, his inward-looking eyes,
The sarcastic, scornful smile on his lips,
The unkempt, matted, grey hair,
The hard, coarse sand-paper hands,
5 Spoke eloquently of the life he had lived.
But I did not mourn for him.

The hammer, the saw and the plane,
These were his tools and his damnation,
His sweat was his ointment and his perfume.
10 He fashioned dining tables, chairs, wardrobes,
And all the wooden loves of colonial life
No, I did not mourn for him.

He built colonial mansions,
Huge, unwieldy, arrogant constructions;
15 But he squatted in a sickly mud-house,
With his children huddled stuntedly
Under the bed-bug bed he shared with Mother.
I could not mourn for him.

I had already inherited
20 His premature old-age look,
I had imbibed his frustration;
But his dreams of freedom and happiness
Had become my song, my love.
So, I could not mourn for him.

25 No, I did not shed any tears;
My father's dead life still lives in me,
He lives in my son, my father,
I am my father and my son,
I will awaken his sleepy hopes and yearnings,
30 But I will not mourn for him,
I will not mourn for me.

QUESTIONS

1 Although this poem records the experience of an individual, does it in any way have significance for everyone?

2 What words or expressions in the poem show the speaker's emotions?

3 From your own understanding of the poem, why did the speaker not want to mourn for his father?

4 What is your reaction to the type of predicament which the poet describes in the poem? Refer to line 26 in answering this question.

Like the Sea and its Waters

Waigwa Wachira

I have seen the sun rise and set
with a volcanic passion of flaming orange
and I have thought of the passion of our sweet love
that once rose and set
5 like the sun in the sky

75

I have seen trees after sunset
getting ready to sleep
and mountains at dusk with purple blankets
and soft clouds of ink;
10 and softly I have thought of you

I have stood on the ferry
in the Indian Ocean
and have breathed
the sweet scented air
15 that God gave to the sea:
and I have thought of the fragrance
of a love that once shone so brightly
like the stars in the sky.

I have sat barefoot
20 on the rocks by the lake
wondering what went wrong
wishing that I could hold you;
knowing that I have lost you;
feeling my thoughts fly
25 like a bird across the sea
on the lonely wings of love far . . . .
far away from home and you.

And as I walk on the sands of a shore
that our feet used to know
30 my eyes hurt with unshed tears;
my soul turning as the wind calls your name
for I miss you desperately and I look for you
with every breath that I take.

If I could touch and hold the sun
35 I'd give it to you
if I could plant flowers in the sand
and make them grow
I would plant them just for you;
for I have kissed you when you cried
40 and tasted the salty blue turbulence of your soul.

And if in my turn
I should give up and die
or simply break down and cry
forgive me lady dear
45 and help me dry my tears
for it is the cry of the fisherman
after the sea is gone.

You are like the sea
and its waters to me
50 and I have loved you dearly;
more dearly than the spoken word can tell.

QUESTIONS

1 What type of poem would you say this is?

2 What does this poem describe? (Explain it in your own words).

3 Can you find instances of exaggeration? What effect does this have on the poem?

4 Write a critical appreciation of this poem, commenting on the imagery and anything else that interests you.

5 How does the poet use rhythm to help us appreciate the subject of the poem?

6 The poet uses images reflecting most of the five human senses. Can you identify and discuss these?

Ngoma*

Yusuf O. Kassam

The drum beats,
And with bare feet and red earth,
Rhythm erupts,
Muscles and drums synchronized.
5 Bodies sweat,
Vigorously,
Glistening round the flickering fire,
Erotic.
The night is long,
10 Drums beat more furiously,
Moving the kaleidoscope of frenzied expressions,
And the pulse outruns the drum beat.
The drums inspired the dancers,
Now the dancers inspire the drummers.
15 No more.
Relax.

Wipe the dust and the sweat.
But the pulse still beats,
Muscles twitch,
20   And drums echo,
All in a hangover of rhythm,
African rhythm.

Ngoma   (title): a symbolic, African traditional drum

QUESTIONS

1 Can you think of another title, using a different way of describing the subject matter in the poem?

2 What is the general mood of the poem?

3 Can you identify the various movements in the poem?

4 What is the meaning of the following lines?
   a) 'Muscles and drums synchronized' (line 4)

   b) 'Moving the kaleidoscope of frenzied expressions' (line 11)

   c) 'And the pulse outruns the drum beat' (line 12)

   d) 'Now the dancers inspire the drummers' (line 14)

Fort Jesus

Amin Kassam

Every day you gaze
Gaze
Gaze out at the boundless ocean
Grim
5   Forbidding
Timeless.
Your battered faded walls
Recall a cruel era
Yet there is grace too
10   Amidst the scars of tragedy
Rock bones carved
Enchanting
Monument to Man's harshness.
You have concealed and preserved

15 Dreadful secrets
    Unrevealed.
    Dissection has wrenched out the past
    Now
    What was past is present
20 The present is the past
    The future is past.

    Nothing remains
    But deathless fascination.

QUESTIONS

1 What effect does the repetition of the word 'gaze' in the first three lines have on the rest of the poem?

2 Comment on the use of personification in this poem.

3 Would you say the poet has been economical or extravagant in his expression of emotion here?

4 What is the symbolic meaning of the following lines:
   (a) 'What was past is present
       The present is the past
       The future is past' (lines 19–21)

   (b) 'Nothing remains
       But deathless fascination.' (lines 22–23)

Kano Plains

Robert Okinyi

    I caught this evening a scene,
    A man supplicating the gods,
    Hands heavenwards,
    Brows knotted,
5   Streams of sorrow along the cheeks,
    Heart distended, yet in fealty to the gods,
    To succour the soil with dew.

    The gods listened to his prayers;
    The arrows of rain began

10 To pierce the fields without pity;
The seeds sprouted and were choked;
The fields that had been baked
Were now blanketed in a canopy of water.

He returned to the gods,
15 Hands heavenwards,
Brows knitted,
Streams of tears along the cheeks,
Heart distended with allegiance to the gods
To dispel the diluvium from the fields.

20 The gods listened to his prayers,
the diluvium began to ebb;
The fields dried up;
The seeds that had been planted choked.
When he returned to the gods
25 For rain, they answered him,
"Since you didn't want rain
We won't give it you again".

QUESTIONS

1 What type of poem is this?

2 How does the poet create the mood in it?

3 What effect does the repetition of certain phrases have upon the poem?

4 Compare this poem with Jared Angira's 'the final appeal' (Page 119) in this anthology. How do the two poems differ from each other? Which one do you prefer and why?

The Dawn

Lillian Ingonga

In the twilight
The first bird sings a melody
To break the darkness silence
The chirping sounds that
5 Drown the fading songs of the crickets!

The morn is here again
Herald the new day born

In the twilight
The first sun-rays
10 Light the still dark grey sky
The deep dark blue sky
Swallows the stars as they
Twinkle, twinkle their last!

The rays in stray
15 The night shadows behind cast

In the young day born
The dew shines on grass blades
Throwing kaleidoscopic rays
The cock crows
20 The sun peeps

From behind the clouds
Starts its pilgrim across the sky

In the morning light
Still wet and grey with mist
25 The bird's song grows loud
The flowers upon beauty display

The dew on fresh blooms
Shines as the bird's song rings

QUESTIONS

1 Which lines in the poem could be called a 'chorus'?

2 What effect does repetition have in this poem?

3 Comment on the rhythm of the poem.

4 How much use does the poet make in this poem of references to colour? What effect does it have?

5 Discuss the use of accumulation of details in this poem.

6 Explain the symbolic significance of the following lines:
  a) 'Throwing kaleidoscopic rays' (line 18)

  b) 'Starts its pilgrim across the sky' (line 22)

  c) 'The dew on fresh blooms' (line 27)

Women Walking At Alice and Trevor's Wedding Or Intermarriage

David Rubadiri

Women walking –
Two women,
A hot bright Kampala afternoon
Busuti swashing
5   Picking wood
On Mulago Hill,
Probably gossiping;
Inwardly telling lies
and truths
10 About their homes and husbands
But always about themselves.

Saint Francis
On Makerere Hill
Stood quiet and still
15 Rocked by organ peals
Tradition knocking at the door
Prejudice rampant
Fear and awe –
Grappling with terror
20 As Alice and Trevor
Walked the path of thunder.

QUESTIONS

1 How appropriate is the title of the poem?

2 What is the economy of expression in this poem intended to reflect?

3 What contradictions does the poet raise in the poem?

4 In what ways does the poet paint a vivid picture of the scene and setting?

Death At Mulago

David Rubadiri

Towers of strength
granite
hard concrete
enduring
5 like life itself.

Up they rise
tall and slender
and around them
white coats flit
10 like the magic they spell.

New Mulago Hospital
– the name shakes –
she stood firmly
on that cool afternoon
15 giving names, tribe and sex,
A woman clad in busuti.

As the fullstop was entered
on a white sheet of paper
a whitecoat gave a nod.

20 Her hands cross her chest
and the message unsaid
crushing granite and concrete
in gushing tears of pain
and a lonely sorrow.

QUESTIONS

1 Discuss in detail the use of personification in this poem.

2 Do you consider the poem angry or sorrowful? Use illustrations from the text.

3 What is the economy of expression in this poem intended to reflect?

4 Explain the relationship between line 19 and the title of the poem.

He passes by me . . . .!

Felix Mnthali

He passes by me
dolled up in the latest fashions,
knee-tight trousers
multi- coloured shirt:
5 he even walks on stilts
to defeat the ravages of time!

Is this the way, I wonder,
is this the way?
greasing our heads
10 as from women's salons
borrowing a face
from an age
out of tune
with its hopes and fears?

15 These are the fixations
of adolescence
with rules made out of puberty
and a game
men will always lose
20 because the rules
are made by rivals.

Why should we borrow
their robes and their speech?
If we learn from them
25 What will they learn
from us?

QUESTIONS

1 What does the first line of the poem imply?

2 How many people is the poet referring to within the poem? What is the significance of this?

3 Comment on the poet's choice of words, bearing in mind their effectiveness.

4 Examine the punctuation marks used in the poem. How do they help us to read the poem sensibly?

Silence in the board-room

Felix Mnthali

. . . . silence
   that weird shape
   of the devil's transit
   en route to nowhere

5 We waited
   knowing that the chairman on arrival
   would reveal nothing
   hide nothing
   that we did not know

10 those stale jokes of yesterday
   would be warmed up
   for to-day's meeting –

   no clues here
   to the traumas of tomorrow;
15 genius and nincompoop
   emerge not
   out of such meetings

   out of the genius
   came only gibberish
20 and the wit of the clown
   became wordy

   we came all the way
   from Nsanje and Karonga
   Nkhota-kota and Mchinji
25 to yawn in our immaculate suits
   and listen to this . . . .
   this gist of nothingness

QUESTIONS

1 What impact does the very first line of the poem create?

2 What interpretation can you give to the whole of the first stanza?

3 What kind of relationship do you think there is between the chairman and the board members?

4 Can you find any instance of satire in this poem?

5 Explain the meaning of the following lines:
   a) 'genius and nincompoop
      emerge not
      out of such meetings' (lines 15–17)

   b) 'out of the genius
      came only gibberish' (lines 18–19)

Farewell to a Volkswagen

Felix Mnthali

As all cars go
you went:
a void reigns
in my life.

5 Together
            we have seen
            rain
            and wind

            the wind that settles on your face
10   like unseen blessings
            from a half-forgotten era

            the wind that covers your body
            like a curse
            from your ancestors

15   the wind that sings in your ears
            like haunted messages
            from the shrine
            of your clan

   Together
20   we have heard noises
            noises
            that split your ear
            like a gunshot
            in the middle of the night
25   noises
            that paralyse your mind
            like desire
            in the wrong place
            at the wrong time

30

Together
        we have seen roads
        roads
        littered with sharp-edged gravel
        like broken china
35   after a midnight carousal
        like ground glass
        after a highway collision
        like the glitter of diamonds
        in a pauper's dream

40 Together
        we have confronted risks
        risks
        of leopards striding across lonely roads
        of pelicans
45   gleaming like angels
        at the heart of darkness
        risks
        of your air filter
        hanging loose
50   in the middle of nowhere
        of red lights flashing across your dashboard
        like lightning
        across a mountain of clouds
        of a leaping heart checked in mid-air
55   like an angry warrior
        in the vice of a peace-maker

Together
        we have inhaled dust
        dust
60   that blocks your nostrils
        scratches your lungs
        chokes your silencer
        into a grinding mill
        and changes us both
65   into *Nyau** dancers!
        together we have inhaled dust

Above all, we have seen roads
        roads hanging
        on plateaux
70   on mountain ranges
        on peaks
        like creepers reaching out for the sun

We have seen roads
flitting to nowhere
75   racing towards a cul-de-sac
like delicate insects
lured by artificial light

We have seen roads
crossing rickety bridges
80   with nails like uncovered teeth
and planks creaking like old beds
supporting young lovers

We have seen
the road to Lunzu Market
85   the road to Ulumba
the road to Kaporo
the road to gloom
to ecstasy
to the future
90 and in these days of shortages
and escalating costs
who would not wish
you were here?

*Nyau   (line 65): traditional Community in Malawi well known
for its traditional dancers.

QUESTIONS

1 What impact does the use of the word 'together' create in the
poem?

2 What mood is created?

3 Are there any elements of *personification* in the poem?

4 What does the poem tell you about the landscape and natural life
within its setting?

5 What do you think the poet is referring to in lines 15–18?

6 Find examples of the poet's use of similes. How effective are
they?

7 What gives the poem its strong rhythm? (Use specific examples
for illustration).

8 Have you noticed anything else about Felix Mnthali's poetic
technique that pleases you as you read the poem?

PART THREE

Twin Ceremony

Richard Ntiru

People gossip as much at funerals as on weddings
(As if to make a sinister equation)
In market places as much as in cathedrals

    where babies are washed of natal innocence
5   unions flattered with lifetime happiness
    all deaths earnestly pronounced untimely. . . .

So it is on this twin ceremony
Indoors a couple pledges to multiply and fill the earth
'Until death do us part'
10 While the gay crowd exchange winks
Wondering if he knows. . . .

    Outside a draped coffin awaits the ultimate
        blackmail – 'dust to dust' –
    As the businesslike gravediggers murmur
15   Puzzlement at the extinction of one with
        mountains
    And wonder why he died so late

High in the sky Nature's nonchalant Eye
Is beaming, sprinkling confetti with the dust of death
20 Unbothered which is the more serious business
I am dazed, drifting into yet another hopeless situation
I can hear echoes of the nuptial pledges
Merging into the words of the Requiem
As I contemplate Nature's Siamese shape. . . .

25   Tomorrow the printed consolation will surely
        come
    As places are appointed for the two parties
    One for a happy and fruitful life on Mother
        Earth's lap
30   Another for eternal rest in Mother Earth's
        peaceful bowels

QUESTIONS

1 Explain the meaning of the title.

2 Can you identify any use of paradox in the poem?

3 Comment on the poet's use of satire in this poem.

4 Can you detect a slight touch of humour 'between the lines' of this poem?

5 What effect do the refrains achieve in the poem?

6 Discuss in detail the critical statements made by the poem.

The function

Richard Ntiru

This was her fourth function.

I still see her,
unreturning the erect chauffeur's grin,
adjusting eyes behind sunglasses,
5 glancing unseeingly at her dazzling wrist,
checking quickly with the goddess of status
– and breathing the sigh of a soul
sagging under the common grief.

Her heartfelt sympathy to the cripples
10 she read to the able-bodied audience,
urging the victims to build the nation
with more and more economic products
"like these you've given me".

As the tape-cutting fingers
15 rise with the solemn delicacy of a surgeon,
her well-protected photogenic gaze
eludes the flattered wooden gapes
and the tape misses the scissors.

A crammed schedule curtailed her pleasure.

20 A bouquet charmed her sight
and she uncovered her eyes
to confront beauty with beauty.
Suddenly she noticed the shrivelled, contorted form
behind the beauty of flowers
25 and collapsed into a heap. . . .

1 What is implied in the following?
   a) 'adjusting eyes behind sunglasses' (line 4)

   b) 'glancing unseeingly at her dazzling wrist' (line 5)

   c) '– and breathing the sigh of a soul
      sagging under the common grief' (lines 7–8)

   d) 'A crammed schedule curtailed her pleasure' (line 19)

2 Comment on the second and third stanzas. Discuss the satire in them.

3 Explain how the last three lines relate to the rest of the poem. Why did the woman collapse?

4 What is Ntiru's attitude towards the woman in the poem? Justify your answer.

Rhythm of the pestle

Richard Ntiru

Listen – listen –
listen to the palpable rhythm
of the periodic pestle,
plunging in proud perfection
5   into the cardial cavity
of maternal mortar
like the panting heart
of the virgin bride
with the silver hymen,
10   or the approaching stamp
of late athleting cows
hurrying home to their bleating calves.

At each succeeding stroke
the grain darts, glad to be scattered
15   by the hard glint
of the pestle's passion.

During the aerial suspension
of the pendent pestle
the twice-asked, twice-disappointed girl

20 thinks of the suitor that didn't come,
of her who dragged her name through ashes
uncleansed by the goat-sacrifice,
of her bridal bed
that vanished with the ephemeral dream,
25 of her twin firstlings
that will never be born,
and her weltering hands
grip, grip, rivet hard
and downright down
30 comes the vengeance pestle.

I have seen the hearth
and the triplets,
but no trace of ash. . . .

Now the grain jumps, reluctantly,
35 each time lower and lower,
smiling the half-white smile
of the teething baby,
glad to be crushed,
glad to be sublimated
40 to the quintessential powder
after the consummation.

In the bananas
the girls dance, singing of one
who saw her father in sleepy drunkenness
45 and confided in the birds of the sky.

Still the perennial pestle
pounds the tribulations of a battered soul
and the caked countenance of an orphaned age
to the intensity and fineness
50 of a powder.

QUESTIONS

1 Comment on the use of alliteration in this poem. What effect
does it create?

2 Explain the meaning of the following lines:
a) 'listen to the palpable rhythm' (line 2)

b) 'the approaching stamp
of late athleting cows' (lines 10–11)

c) 'of her bridal bed
   that vanished with the ephemeral dream' (lines 23–24)

d) 'after the consummation' (line 41)

3 In your own words, explain what you understand by the third
  stanza.

4 How does the poet develop the subject matter of the poem?

The Guilt of Giving

Laban Erapu

You've seen that heap of rags
That pollutes the air-conditioned
City Centre,
That louse that creeps about
5 In the clean core of sophistication;
You've seen him waylay his betters
And make them start –
Especially when they have no change.

You recall the day you came upon him
10 And were startled by his silent presence
Intruding into your preoccupation:
You hurled a coin
Which missed the mark
And rolled into the gutter
15 Where he groped for it
With a chilling grotesque gratitude
That followed you down the street.
You dived into the nearest shop
To escape the stare
20 Of the scandalised crowd
That found you guilty
Of recalling attention
To the impenetrable patience
They had learnt not to see.

QUESTIONS

1 What is the meaning of the title?

94

2 What does this poem describe? (Explain it in your own words).

3 What feelings does the poet show for the person he refers to in the first line of the poem?

4 Explain the meaning of the following lines or expressions:
   a) 'that heap of rags' (line 1)

   b) 'That louse that creeps about
      In the clean core of sophistication' (lines 4–5)

   c) 'With a chilling grotesque gratitude' (line 16)

   d) 'Of the scandalised crowd' (line 20).

A Taxi Driver on his Death

Timothy Wangusa

When with prophetic eye I peer into the future
I see that I shall perish upon this road
Driving men that I do not know.
This metallic monster that I now dictate,
5 This docile elaborate horse,
That in silence seems to simmer and strain,
Shall surely revolt some tempting day.
Thus I shall die; not that I care
For any man's journey,
10 Nor for proprietor's gain,
Nor yet for love of my own.
Not for these do I attempt the forbidden limits,
For these defy the traffic-man and the cold cell.
Risking everything for the little little more.
15 They shall say, I know, who pick up my bones,
'Poor chap, another victim to the ruthless machine' –
Concealing my blood under the metal.

QUESTIONS

1 Which of these is the dominant sentiment in the poem: hate or resignation? Illustrate your answer with reference to particular words or phrases.

2 Would you characterize this poem as public or as private protest? Defend your choice.

3 Explain the following lines in the poem:
   a) 'When with prophetic eye I peer into the future' (line 1)

   b) 'This metallic monster that I now dictate' (line 4)

   c) 'This docile elaborate horse' (line 5)

   d) 'Not for these do I attempt the forbidden limits' (line 12)

4 What qualities of oral poetry are evident in this poem?

I Met a Thief

Austin Bukenya

On the beach, on the coast,
Under the idle, whispering coconut towers,
Before the growling, foaming, waves,
I met a thief who guessed I had
5 An innocent heart for her to steal.

She took my hand and led me under
The intimate cashew boughs which shaded
The downy grass and peeping weeds.
She jumped and plucked the nuts for me to suck;
10 She sang and laughed and pressed close.

I gazed; her hair was like the wool of a mountain
                                    sheep,
Her eyes, a pair of brown-black beans floating in milk.
Juicy and round as plantain shoots
15 Her legs, arms and neck;
And like wine-gourds her pillowy breasts;
Her throat uttered fresh banana juice:
Matching her face – smooth and banana-ripe.

I touched – but long before I even tasted,
20 My heart had flowed from me into her breast;
And then she went – High and South –
And left my carcase roasting in the fire she'd lit.

QUESTIONS

1 What is the implication of the poem's title?

2 What is this poem really about, in terms of everyday life?

3 What does the poem tell you about the setting?

4 Comment on the poet's use of imagery and its effectiveness.

The Struggle

Kalungi Kabuye

We live in each other's pockets,
envying our neighbours' cooking pots,
while we leave our toes in our shoes
to be gnawed at by little ticklish bugs
5 of laziness, drug-addiction and drunkenness.

in the beer bars we struggle to impress,
while others work to suppress us,
treating us like little flies and fleas
which produce noises only to be ignored.

10 Who called you great, you?
he meant you're a goat.
they call me clever
saying I'm a bin-cover,
a rubbish tip in the city heap.

15 then a city councillor calls me
to the King's Palace, I smile with content,
but there, I am no more than a common beggar
smelling of commonplace liquor.
you dress in morning suit with a bow tie,
20 but you pass for a beggar

drinking local punch seated on a bench,
not in the palace, but in the commoner's trench:
you were in a dream in a lousy bed.

QUESTIONS

1 Is the poem serious, or is it comic?

2 What other title might you suggest for this poem? Why?

3 What contradictions does the poem bring out?

4 What makes this poem satirical?

Rain

David Kihazo

A bundle of rain
Anywhere, when it rains.
Understanding this
Is meaningful life
5 To a mind once hopeless.

In my mind,
Thin threads of raindrops
Fall from the sky,
Confident about the terminus.
10 Aware of each other's competitive nature
Yet, for the same speed, unaware;
Strong wind sometimes
Diverts the bundle to diverse objects:
Roof tops,
15 Balcony,
Grass and tree-leaves
Where destructive hopelessness dwells.

Same speed,
Same thread-thinnness
20 Where all reign as Gods
Or just common raindrops;
Balm of hope,
Meaningful to a mind once hopeless.

QUESTIONS

1 Read the poem very carefully. What interpretation do you give to the first stanza?

2 What feelings does the poet show for rain? How does he communicate them?

3 What is his intention with regard to his expectations of society?

4 Does the poem suggest that there is hope for the future?

Lead Kindly Dark

David Kihazo

Darkened by a path
that needs light,
Extinguished daily by dazzlers;
NOTHING,
5   We are dust
That can't be cleaned
As we are dazzled
By that in dust

10   and
                     we
                     are
                     back
                     to
15   O.

QUESTIONS

1 What is your reaction to the structure of the poem?

2 What is the implication of the title in relationship to the whole
poem?

3 What is the deeper meaning of lines 5–8?

4 What do you think are the feelings of the poet at the end of the
poem?

Not All At Once

David Kihazo

Mother and child;
Let them,
Let them be, grow. . . .

                (I would not have children,
5   I am afraid to bring children into
                this world.
                Oh, I am so tired, I am so tired,

99

                I wish I could lie down somewhere
                and sleep
10   and never wake up, any more).

        (Who shall tell the terrors of the nights
        to the young maiden and child?)

        Mother and child;
        Such purity of heart,
15   Such innocence,
        Such all knowing ignorance
        Of mother safely refusing
        To blame
        Encourages them to
20   Do with improvisations
        Dismembers me, wrathfully,
        From a coterie of unnatural burdens;
        What did we lose?
        What do we lack?
25   What forces us into deprivation,
        Destitution?
        Mock sympathy
        Reveals the other and I:
        We outsavage savages.

QUESTIONS

1 Who do you think the poet is addressing in the first three lines
of the poem?

2 What contribution does the refrain (lines 4–12) make to the
meaning of the poem?

3 Explain the following lines within the context of the poem:
   a) 'Such all knowing ignorance
      Of mother safely refusing
      To blame' (lines 16–18)

   b) 'Dismembers me, wrathfully,
      From a coterie of unnatural burdens' (lines 21–22)

   c) 'Mock sympathy
      Reveals the other and I:
      We outsavage savages.' (lines 27–29)

4 What is the underlying meaning of the questions that the poet
poses in the last stanza?

100

The Motoka

Theo Luzuka

You see that Benz sitting at the rich's end?
Ha! That motoka is motoka
It belongs to the Minister for Fairness
Who yesterday was loaded with a doctorate
5 At Makerere with whisky and I don't know what
Plus I hear the literate thighs of an undergraduate.

You see those market women gaping their mouths?
The glory of its inside has robbed them of words,
I tell you the feather seats the gold steering
10 The TV the radio station the gear!
He can converse with all world presidents
While driving in the back seat with his darly
Between his legs without the driver seeing a thing! ha!
                    ha! ha!
15 Look at the driver chasing the children away
They want to see the pistol in the door pocket
Or the button that lets out bullets from the machine
Through the eyes of the car – sshhhhhhhhhhhhhhhhhh!
Let's not talk about it.

20 But I tell you that motoka can run
It sails like a lyato, speeds like a swallow
And doesn't know anyone stupid on its way
The other day I heard –
But look at its behind, that mother of twins!

25 A – ah! That motoka is motoka
You just wait, I'll tell you more
But let me first sell my tomatoes.

QUESTIONS

1 Comment on the tone of the poem.

2 Who is the speaker in the poem and who is he/she addressing?

3 In what ways is this poem a good example of the effectiveness of free verse?

4 'Ha! That motoka is motoka' (line 2) What do you understand by this expression? What effect does the repetition of it in line 25 have upon the poem?

5 Which other expressions used in this poem are striking to you? In what ways?

6 What effect does line 23 have within the context of the poem?

To the Childless

Kittobbe

You are the cold nests
In which the migrant bird lays no eggs
In which it never enters to brood;

You are the fruits that ripen, rot
5 And the wind blows you down
Dropping with a dead thud;
You are the ever cold hearths
In abandoned homesteads
In which the ghosts bathe the cold ashes
10 Your twin breasts
The two hearth stones that never support the Black
Mother Pot.

Your wombs incommunicado with Earth
Shame, entombing an eternal void:
Mere beehives of drones
15 Encasements of belied watersheds –
Ever drying along the timescape
A spit into the angry bonfire;
You are the last breath that bubbled up God's throat.

And when the last breath is squeezed out of your chest;
20 And a needle is driven into the crust of your head
When your thumbs and last fingers
and tongue and testicles are mutilated
And a dead march escorts your coffin
And the last nail hammered into your tomb
25 Then know that
Your after-life rides on frothy crests of whirlwinds
Haunting only the insensible anthills.

102

1 What is the mood of the poem?

2 In what category can you place this poem?

3 Who is the speaker addressing?

4 Find examples of the poet's use of metaphor. How effective are they?

5 In your own words, state what you think the poet means in the last stanza of the poem.

6 Do you think there is any deeper meaning in this poem or is it a straightforward presentation of the subject matter?

Being

John Ruganda

Once it was the pain of emptiness;
The yawning of the unpossessed I ˎ
Or of possessing drifting shadows:
Waters drip dropping
5 Through a sieve.

Then it was you, you
Strolling above the herd of absurdities
Unbending, untouched, unaffected;
But breezing in to me faster than dawn,
10 And deeper than the hollow depths.

Now these cruel nights!
It is the phantoms of your presence
Tormenting, chiding and consoling;
Like Him who pains and pleases –
15 Seated far above,
Fainter than the moon's melodies,
Yet nearer than breath.

Gone are the fears of tomorrow
Of being in a jostling crowd alone
20 Blind, deaf and dumb.
And in come the thrillings of delight,
Of being when one already is.

1 In what category can you place this poem?

2 What does the exclamation mark in line 11 tell us of the feeling of the poet concerning the main idea contained in the poem?

3 What does this poem tell us of the poet's view of the relationship between the living and the dead?

4 Identify any *three* images. Show that you understand them and comment on their suitability.

Brotherly Advice

Raymond Ntalindwa

Easy, easy brother,
Stop haranguing your elder brother,
Stoop down from your clouds, accept courtesy
Corrosive tongue tags you to hostility.

5 Easy, easy brother,
Put brakes to cascades of breaking relations
Cracking and creaking at every joint,
Aggressive squeaks sketch your bestiality.

Easy, easy brother,
10   Given ability,
A slight thought will prove no iota of
Neither truth nor honesty in your
      Ill-advised
      Ill-thought out
15   Outbursts.
Mischief cheapens your stage-management.

Easy, easy brother,
Look back with sincerity,
Examine your present behaviour
20 Your unwaning, deliberate tricks emitting myopia
     Could be
     your burial myrrh.

Easy, easy brother,
Shrug not your shoulders comically,
25 Dilate not your sinister eyes.
Relax, Botha: dialogue is the causeway, or else . . .

Underrate not your elder brother.

QUESTIONS

1 What effect does the repetition of the words 'Easy, easy brother' have upon the poem?

2 Who do you think is being referred to as the 'elder brother?' (lines 2 and 27).

3 Explain the meaning of the following lines:
   a) 'Corrosive tongue tags you to hostility' (line 4)

   b) 'Aggressive squeaks sketch your bestiality' (line 8)

   c) 'Mischief cheapens your stage-management' (line 16)

   d) 'Your unwaning, deliberate tricks emitting myopia' (line 20).

4 What are the underlying issues in the poem?

The Money-Changers

Richard S. Mabala

Dreamed my way to church
Church built of coloured paper
On silver-coated foundations
Normal unintelligible rumble
5 Of muttered prayers
Barely audible above
The rustle of notes
And the clink of coins
Strange prayer indeed!

10 Our Father who art in – CLINK –
hallowed be thy – CLINK –
Thy – CLINK – come
Thy will be – CLINK –
On earth as it is in heaven.
15 Give us this day our daily – CLINK –
And forgive us our – CLINK –
As we – CLINK – them that trespass against us
And lead us – CLINK – into – CLINK –
But – CLINK CLINK CLINK – evil
20 A – CLINK – .

It was really a magnificent sight
Enough to inspire the most hardened sinner

But I couldn't help trembling
And looking over my shoulder
25 Wondering
When
We would be driven out
With a whip.

QUESTIONS

1 Identify the use of *onomatopoeia* in this poem. What overall effect does it have on the poem?

2 How relevant is the title of the poem?

3 Using your own words, explain the meaning of the first three lines of the poem.

4 What makes this poem satirical?

5 Explain the *allusion* the poet makes in the last stanza within the context of the poem.

Question

Richard S. Mabala

For whom do we write?
Self-appointed guardians of the people's conscience
Arrogant in our ability
To perceive
5 Diagnose
Describe
Prescribe
Trapped by our faith in a writer's power to change,
Do we have the right to claim such power?
10 Or are we just another clan of futile dreamers
Aware maybe of contradictions?
Or mere spectators
Screaming advice
From the cushioned seats
15 Of the covered stands
But unheard above the general roar
And safe in our seats
Impotent to effect any change?

The Ways Of The World

Richard S. Mabala

I watched her at the bus stop
White blouse swelling
Before the impatient push
Of breasts eager to be free;
5   Orange skirt billowing provocatively
Under the silken caress
Of the harbour breeze
Eyes flashing with life
Thirsting to drink deep
10 Of the springs of life
I watched her,
Swallowed hard,
But went quickly on my way,
For she was but a Secondary student.

15 I would have forgotten her
But I saw her again that night
Glowing in the soft light of Mpkani Bar,
Six inches taller
Wide trousers clinging possessively
20 To the youthful thrust of her buttocks
Before dropping to mask the raised heels.
She was transformed!
I wouldn't have recognised her
But for those eyes
25 So provocatively thirsty.
With a pang of jealousy
I glanced at her partner
And choked into my glass –
My father!

30 Trousers fraying dangerously
Before the onslaught of his swollen belly
Sweat dripping from his double chin
Mouth twisted in a grimace
Of drunken desire.
35 The shocking contrast was too great;
I faded into the shadows
And sorrowing went my way.

Then yesterday
I saw her again at the bus stop.
40 Dress hanging loosely
From her broken body.
Stomach swelling grotesque
And those beautiful eyes,
Lifeless now,
45 Gazing unseeing
In dumb protest at what the world has done to her.

Oh! What are we doing to our daughters?

QUESTIONS

1 Can you *see* in your mind's eye the scenes that the poet is
describing? What words make these pictures clear to you?

2 What bearing does line 29 have on the rest of the poem?

3 What are the various feelings of the poet through the poem?

Groaning for Burial

Felix Mnthali

Things will get worse
before they get better –
our third of the tripartite globe
spins on its misery
5 not all of it of our own making
no doubt,
but we must stoop and wash
in the blood of innocents

executed at dawn
10 we must lie down and share
the clammy numbness of the floors
to which men are condemned
without charges and therefore
without trial

15 in the important corridors
of sweet diplomacy
you can hear men talk
of an 'ideological vacuum'
and 'inter-tribal warfare'
20 they talk of things
and not of men

Look back in shame, look back
to the Pan African Congress of 1948
to the Bandung Conference
25 on Afro-Asian solidarity;
look back in shame
to the rainbow of dawn
now lost in the garish haze
of coups, counter-coups
30 and endless detentions

Black stands for the people:
green is the beauty of their land:
red is the blood we spill
to regain the land –
35 but what have we gained
'with carrion men
groaning for burial?'

We wake up wondering
into what insects
40 we are going to be changed
and the corrugated joy of our lives
has now been mangled
beyond recognition

Of course, we had wanted the land
45 as it was
with hopes and loyalties
firmly glued
to the beauty of dawn
where little lambs would frisk
50 in the summer of their prime

and lions would fret and growl
in the seamless cage of the rule of law

no, not this sunless desert
where carrion men
55 groan for burial.

QUESTIONS

1 What is the mood of the poem? How is it created?

2 What does the poet mean by the following expressions:
   a) 'our third of the tripartite globe' (line 3)

   b) 'the clammy numbness of the floors
       to which men are condemned' (lines 11–12)

   c) 'with carrion men
       groaning for burial' (lines 36–37)

   d) 'and the corrugated joy of our lives' (line 41)

3 What are the poet's feelings in lines 20–21?

4 Put what the poem says into your own words. (Make sure you keep
within the context).

A Leopard Lives in a Muu Tree

Jonathan Kariara

A leopard lives in a Muu tree
Watching my home
My lambs are born speckled
My wives tie their skirts tight
5 And turn away –
Fearing mottled offspring.
They bathe when the moon is high
Soft and fecund
Splash cold mountain stream water on their nipples
10 Drop their skin skirts and call obscenities.

I'm besieged
I shall have to cut down the muu tree
I'm besieged
I walk about stiff
15 Stroking my loins
A leopard lives outside my homestead
Watching my women
I have called him elder, the one-from-the-same-womb
He peers at me with slit eyes
20 His head held high
My sword has rusted in the scabbard.
My wives purse their lips
When owls call for mating
I'm besieged
25 They fetch cold mountain water
They crush the sugar cane
But refuse to touch my beer horn.
My fences are broken
My medicine bags torn
30 The hair on my loins is singed
The upright post at the gate has fallen
My women are frisky
The leopard arches over my homestead
Eats my lambs
35 Resuscitating himself.

QUESTIONS

1 Would you say the poet has been economical or extravagant in his expression of emotion here?

2 In what ways does the poet make a distant scene a little more familiar?

3 What are the dominant images in this poem and what is their significance?

4 Poetry frequently reflects the social or economic life of a community. What kind of community is portrayed here?

5 Explain the implication of the following lines:
  a) 'I walk about stiff
     Stroking my loins' (lines 14–15)

  b) 'My sword has rusted in the scabbard'(line 21)

111

c) 'My wives purse their lips
   When owls call for mating' (lines 22–23)

d) 'The hair on my loins is singed' (line 30)

The Desert

Amin Kassam

hear my burning cry o heavens!
hear the lament
of a disillusioned soul
whose footprints weave drunkenly
5 across the desert floor
you have seen me trudging
across the sands
through whirling storms
staggering over dunes
10 gasping with thirst
you have seen my steps falter
in oozing sand
you have seen me crawl towards
dry scintillant water
15 and yet beneath your relentless gaze
i still plead,
plead for but a drop!

even the cactus raises hinged arms
aloft in supplication.
20 is there no emotion in you o heavens,
no compassion
must i believe we are robots
that the spark of humanity is lost
then i am not alone
25 for many have crossed this floor
many have looked to the garden
with hopeful despair
as though at a mirage
and wept
30 hear my whisper o heavens
before i fall
i have not the strength
to thunder forth my words

112

in this land ravaged of hope
35 where bleached bones
seem to say
despair of escape . . . .
perhaps there is no return.

QUESTIONS

1 What type of poem is this?

2 What is its tone?

3 Is there any element of personification in the poem?

4 What images are there in the poem? How do they enhance the
poet's meaning?

5 What feelings does the poet arouse in you, the reader? Explain
clearly with illustrations from the poem.

Maji Maji

Yusuf O. Kassam

Sitting on a stool outside his mud hut,
The mzee scratched his head in a slow motion,
Trying to recall.
His dim grey eyes quiveringly stared into the distance
5 And with a faint faltering voice he spoke
Of the wind that stirred sinister feelings,
Of the leaves that rustled with foreboding,
Of the men who talked of deliverance and freedom,
And of the warriors who pledged to fight.
10 Then he paused and snuffed some tobacco
"The Germans – " He shook his head and shuddered:
"Yes, they came – with guns, to be sure –
Many guns."
His glance slowly shifted in a broken semi-circle
15 At each of the few listeners who squatted on the
ground.
He pointed to the distant hills on his right:
"For many days,

They resounded with drum-beats and frenzied cries;
Then with the spirits of alien ancestors
20   They thundered with strange unearthly sounds."
Placing both his hands on his head,
He looked down on the earth and pronounced,
"They fired bullets, not water, no, not water."
He looked up, with a face crumpled with agony,
25   And with an unsteady swing of his arm, he said,
"Dead, we all lay dead."
While the mzee paused, still and silent,
His listeners gravely looked at each other
Seeming to echo his last words in chorus.
30   Finally, exhausted, he sighed,
"The Germans came and went,
And for many long years
No drums beat again,"

QUESTIONS

1 What role does 'the mzee' (line 2) play in the poem?

2 What contribution does the use of dialogue make to the poem?

3 Choose *one* line from the poem which gives you the impression of how long the mzee's story took.

4 What do you gather from the poem about the listeners' reactions to the story?

5 Can you find *one* instance of exaggeration? What effect does this have on the poem?

6 How would you interpret the last line of the poem in relationship to line 18?

Epistle to Uganda

Leteipa Ole Sunkuli

Children will bear
On their shoulders
The murderers of their mothers

The murderers of their fathers
5   In a treacherous embrace

Ill-clad, tough-faced juveniles
Bearing the mute agents of death
            Will strut
                    The streets
10   Of the City
            Driven
                    By wild and innocent revenge
Against the unseen
Against Authority
15 To avenge their parents' death

When like flies they swarm the city
There will be no childhood
The innocence of childhood will be no more
Even 5-year-olds will be soldiers
20 They will be in the city by hundreds
To stand against those
Who wrenched childhood from them.

QUESTIONS

1 What is the meaning of the poem's title?

2 From the context of the poem, what striking things have happened to give rise to the poem?

3 Comment on the irony in line 5 in relationship of the whole poem.

4 What effect does the repetition of the word 'childhood' (lines 17, 18 and 22) have upon the poem?

5 Does the poem suggest that there is hope for the future?

The Ahs and Ohs of Admiration

Kwendo Opanga

The red on her lips arrested many an eye
But the glittering ear rings wrested them from

her lips to her ears
Only for a blinding reflected ray to summon
5 them to her neck
Almost immediately a golden shine grabbed
them and fixed them on her head.

Her hair was not black, was never black
it was dyed yellow a week, red a week
10 and brown a week

She was never in a hurry, hers was a slow
walk
Her feet, it seemed, were forever looking for
the best pad on which to land
15 Her hands, it appeared, were always looking
for something, somebody, to hold on for support
Her head never ever rested, it was now
turning left, then right, forward and back
and her eyes were searchy.

20 Then, there was her smile
It was forever rehearsed
There was her voice
It was always learned and re-learned
Always according to the latest star of the
25 silver screen –

It is indeed expensive to win the ahs
and ohs of admiration from the many pretenders
But the descendants of Eve have limitless
patience and time.

QUESTIONS

1 Read the poem carefully. What is the significance of the title?

2 This poem is a very *visual* one: it could have been written by a painter. Find evidence for this statement.

3 What makes this poem satirical?

4 What bearing does the last stanza have on the rest of the poem?

116

Armanda

Jared Angira

Armanda was a well-meaning lass:
Read anthropology at college,
Danced the whisky on the rocks,
Smoked Dunhill to the hills,
5　And drove men off their heads
By her beauty, the beauty of the peahen.

Armanda was a well-meaning lass:
Hated the kitchen and its bureaucracy,
Abhorred the cards and the bridge,
10　Disliked the chess and the radio,
Screamed at the telly,
And frowned at the Scrabble.

Armanda was a well-meaning lass
Until she turned the apple-cart
15　Marrying the semi-paralytic Ray;
That was 'true love', so she said,
And insisted that the crutches
Were part of Ray that sent her on heat
And tickled her most!

20　Armanda was a well-meaning lass
Until they flew to distant lands
To sow the seeds of *happiness*;
In her well meaning, thank God,
There is hell expanding each day.
25　She led him to the bank
Laying all the millions
Into Armanda who missed nothing
And misses nobody.

In her well meaning, thank heavens,
30　There is hell, heating each day.
She led him to the orthopaedics
Recommending a plastic thigh.
Henceforth, Ray too could dance the tango
And converse at cocktail parties
35　All without the 'tickling' crutches.

There is no perfection in this world:
The surgery a disaster,
Ray regressed to the wheelchair

And Armanda confined to sympathy.
40 The well-meaning eyes went shy
And the sight of love
Became the sight of pity.
Safe with the account,
Safe with the pills,
45 Suddenly she qualified as judge
To judge the quick and the slow.
Life between two people
Is but plastic association
When one is resigned to pity
50 When one must always give
And another ever receive,
If I must dress you up
And push your wheelchair,
You too must dress me up
55 And drive me to the beach
A meaningful marriage.

One evening as the wind blew
A piece of paper came floating
In the wind and as it rested on Ray's lap
60 He read what he had always expected one day,
        'Goodbye love, goodbye Ray,
        I thought I could change it
        But I have failed
        And I've flown home.'
65 And Ray never thought
Of his millions in her name.

QUESTIONS

1 What type of poem would you say this is?

2 What effect does the repetition of the first line of the poem in the other stanzas have?

3 If you were to perform this poem, what would you do to dramatize its meaning?

4 What does the poem say about human values?

5 Can you find instances of exaggeration? What effect does this have on the poem?

6 Have you noticed anything about Angira's poetic technique that pleases you as you read the poem?

The final appeal

Jared Angira

I have been into the chapel many times
With good intention, as their representative

I have sought audience with god, for those ten years
To represent their wishes, their grievances, I have failed

5 In any case I have a mission to fulfill
To say that they have prayed in private
They have given the little they had in the collection dish
(They were warned never to mention)
And they are still soaring the streets, still searching
10 In desperation, for a staple tuber . . . .

Last night, seated on the chairman's seat
(The high stool at the counter)
I noted their complaints, since they cannot give the
      ultimatum,
15 And to which we hoorayed with the bottle
Still yearning for an alternative outlet
For they could not kick me out, the mission is spiky

As the spokesman, I now seek guidance O lord
Upon a point of misunderstanding
20 Will you really descend, dear god,
From your ivory tower up there
Descend from Mount Hermon to the unchosen

Will you really listen to their grievances
Presented in broken pidgin english-french-spanish
25 Will you listen to genuine cases that have been pending
Of those whose inner limbs you dismembered in the
                        going
Of those whose wombs you endowed with snakes
Of those who were deprived of intestines
30 Of those whom you told to watch and listen

O lord, will you descend and address the workers

Revive their breaths with droplets of dew
At least let me earn my dues for serving some
   purposeful course.

QUESTIONS

1 Who do you think the poet is referring to in the first two stanzas of the poem?

2 What type of poem do you think this is?

3 Are there any elements of satire in the poem?

4 Comment on the structure of the poem. What effect does it create?

5 Explain the following within the context of the poem:

  a) 'a staple tuber' (line 10)

  b) 'hoorayed with the bottle' (line 15)

  c) 'the mission is spiky' (line 17)

  d) 'Of those whose inner limbs you dismembered in the going' (line 26)

The letters

Jared Angira

You have written me
     six letters
I saw in them knots
     to be untied
5 First was, merely
     "yours". . . .
I liked that
     though I never owned you
In any case
10   we'd danced the tango
Not that
     we possessed each other
Then you wrote,
     "yours very truly"

15 Not that "very"
          meant much more
          than "truly"
But how true were you
          when in the night
20 You trailed in my farm
          and uprooted the seedling?
I saw less hypocrisy
          in the third letter
When you said
25   "your beloved"
You were not the first
          to misuse words
And I knew you belied
          all the flash from the hills
30 But when you signed
          "yours faithfully"
I got concerned
          for when we danced
The cuban marimba
35   entwining each other
There was no gesture
          of faith
Indeed I saw you raise
          your arm
40 To cast that vote
          of no confidence
                    against me.
And you keep varying
          your tactics
45 May be
          it's business
                    "yours sincerely"
When sincerely you knew
          we had no dialogue
50 Nor sincerity.
And when
          in your final letter
You ended
          "yours affectionately"
55 I knew
          the anachronism
For it is you
          Who was to effect
                    my crucifixion

1 Is the poem serious, or is it comic?

2 What impression do you get about the poet's attitude towards letters?

3 What is the poet's opinion about the sender of the letters referred to in the poem?

4 What comment can you make about the way in which the poet develops his theme?

By the Seaside

A. D. Amateshe

The waves slowly rise high
towards the crowded beaches
bringing along with them
the broken parts of the Orient.

5 Strides away from the retreat,
beneath the whispering palms
which lure the coconut-climber
Kanamai watches the bewildered strangers.

The roaring waves still rise –
10 this time towards the scorching sun
to catch the swimmers unawares:
Hurriedly, they seek refuge in the sand.

They hide in mounds of sand
to escape the agony of others;
15 they turn their backs to the vultures,
fearing a sharp bend in the course.

They, who derive solace
from the immortal embrace at the horizon,
lie in pools of sweat
20 eagerly watching the west-bound sun.

Gradually, the deep blue turns red –
memories of blood from broken hearts
flowing into the common pool of misery –
red smouldering in blistered souls:

25 Why do we holiday on beaches

to expose our nudity to strange winds?
Why do we partake of the salty waters
not remembering the oriental cremations?

QUESTIONS

1 Why do you think the poet refers to the holiday-makers as 'bewildered' strangers? (line 8)

2 Discuss the irony in the second and third stanzas of the poem.

3 What is the implication of the fourth stanza?

4 Explain the meaning of the following:
   a) 'from the immortal embrace at the horizon' (line 18)

   b) '. . . the deep blue turns red' (line 21)

   c) 'red smouldering in blistered souls' (line 24)

   d) '. . . the oriental cremations' (line 28)

5 What comment can you make about the use of rhetoric in the last stanza?

The Anniversary

A. D. Amateshe

At the mid of the memorable night
we watched the Union Jack,
in a momentary darkness,
slowly coming down into oblivion:

5   Wiped the tears
       of several decades of suppression;
       recalled the terror
       of a colonial past;
       hugged the warmth of the New Day,
10   long-awaited by millions of patriots.

We watched the flag of Mwangaza
steadily, stoically going up
the heroic post of freedom
amidst joyful sighs of relief –

123

15   radiating smiles from those
        whose lives had been dented
        by the national struggle;
        deafening cheers from a people
        whose history had been trampled upon
20   by alien forces of destruction.

But dawn unveiled our eyes
to the labyrinth of self-rule;
each one of us no longer part
of the momentous FREEDOM SQUARE

25   different paths of tribalism
        through waterlogged valleys of greed;
        slippery slopes of nepotism
        down the dungeons of power-struggle,
        crawling into tunnels of sabotage
30   for we wanted a jungle of our own!

Now, we stand firm,
several years of untold challenges,
to build a nation – *ONE* in all, *ALL* in one
unrivalled by our enemies' model:

35   the ideal of a tranquil state
        must not be dwarfed by decadence
        or a selfish ego in foreign aid;
        we must stretch our gifted hands
        from the stronghold of our hearts
40   to those who yawn at gaping thresholds.

Twelfth-december-nineteen-eighty-eight:
our minds rove to the misty beginning
scan the annals of toil and tolerance
to take stock of the distance –

45   we have come a long, long way
        from the days of imported values
        stuffed down our yelling throats
        to the Nyayo Era of Vision;
        we now sing a New Anthem
50   weighing our strength against TOMORROW.

QUESTIONS

1 What type of poem would you say this is?

124

2 What purpose do you think the pattern of the stanzas serves?

3 Discuss the use of imagery and its overall effect in the poem.

4 How do the speaker's feelings change during the poem?

5 Write a poem or prose passage describing the kind of future the speaker hopes for.

Mother of Children

A. D. Amateshe

She rummages through her life,
for what the children will eat;
from the break of dawn to dusk
she juggles with the little at hand
5   to feed the spilling household.

Her hands, blistered with labour
till the unyielding piece of land;
from the start of rains to drought
she gleans the grains of hardship
10 to fill the barrel of tolerance.

Her feet, roughened by treks,
walk the unending paths of struggle;
from the turn of day to the turn of night
the endless search for water
15 takes her beyond the emaciated hills.

Through the wilderness of the plain
her mind wonders about the man
long gone with the hunting season;
her melodious voice fills the air
20 bringing hope to the sullen children.

Daughter of the Toiling Clan,
donor of cattle to your father's homestead,
the cocks are crowing for you
to get up from your rugged bed
25 for another hardening day.

I watch your youngest suckling
the same breasts the others suckled,

my eyes fill with tears of admiration:
your courage, your devotion,
30 your patience for biting questions –

What happened to our father?
Why do you always sing
songs from an 'unburdened' heart,
soothing us all to a 'painless' sleep?
35 When do you rest mama?

Mother of children,
all the yesterdays built on your Motherhood,
listen to the song I sing to you
before the final blow from old age,
40 for I too am your child –

needing your motherly care,
fireside stories full of wisdom,
the readiness to sacrifice for the sake of all,
and your ability to out-live to-day,
45 waiting for the sun to rise again.

QUESTIONS

1 What are the poet's feelings towards 'Mother of Children'?

2 Do you consider the poet's use of the technique of *setting* adequate or overdone? Support your answer with references to the text.

3 What does this poem tell us, by implication, about what is expected of a married woman in an African society?

4 Explain the implications of the following expressions:
   a) 'She gleans the grains of hardship
       to fill the barrel of tolerance' (lines 9–10)

   b) '. . . beyond the emaciated hills' (line 15)

   c) 'donor of cattle to your father's homestead' (line 22)

   d) 'all the yesterdays built on your Motherhood' (line 37)

5 What do we call the kind of questions asked in the seventh stanza, and what is their effect?

6 Explain the relationship between line 40 and the title of the poem.

7 Would you say the poet has been economical or extravagant in his expression of emotion here?

8 What impact do the last two lines have on the poem?

Flight No. BA-067

A. D. Amateshe

>   Seated by the side window
> I see London dwarfed
> by the Nairobi-bound plane –
>
> I try to bring Wood Green
> 5 into the whirlwind of my mind
> but all I remember
> is the fateful day
> of sixth October in Tottenham
> when black and white
> 10 strangled each other
> in the streets.
>
> Earphones
> cut through my head
> as I nervously listen
> 15 to the foreign slipstream –
> 'The people that you never get to love' –
> repeatedly hitting at my conscience
> while I thought of home:
>
> When
> 20 will I shake hands
> with the mother of my children?
>
> When
> will I hold my own images
> in my winter-frozen hands?
>
> 25 But my thoughts are snapped
> by the terrible noise:
> the noise of the propellors
> through the thick clouds;
> the shrill voice of the commentator
> 30 through the chilly chambers;

the rumble of flushing toilets –
all in one reaching my cogged ears.

Ten hours in the skies,
belted on an 'unsafe' seat,
35 thousands of feet above the ground,
hundreds of miles per hour,
I anxiously long for the landing.

QUESTIONS

1 Which words or lines in the poem suggest the passing of time? How do they do so?

2 Briefly describe the meaning of assonance. In this connection, read the poem aloud, listening to your own voice, and find at least one place in the poem where the poet uses assonance. What effect does it have?

3 What bearing does line 16 have on the rest of the poem? And what is your interpretation of the whole theme?

4 What sort of atmosphere does the poem have? How is this atmosphere created?

To the Shameless One

Francis Imbuga

Shameless one ask my clansmen
And you'll be shown the rivers of tears
Whose source is the Chief's homestead,
A constant flow of black sorrow.

5 Ask our neighbours
And you'll be shown the stumps of fallen trees
Whose branches and leaves
Once brought much shade to the Chief's stool.

But now, every year without exception
10 Our rivers of sorrow sweep the ashes
From the murdered trees into the swamp of graves
Beneath the valleys of our memories.

Now you've chosen the trunk itself.
Yes, you've taken my husband's shadow
15 And hidden it behind the future
Destroying the very well that watered your evil thirst.

Tell me shameless one,
Did you not twice think
When you killed your best hand
20 And beckoned your own death with your worst?

QUESTIONS

1 Comment on the structure of the poem.

2 What is its general atmosphere?

3 Who is the speaker in the poem?

4 Does it have any elements of 'oral-ness'?

5 If you were to perform this poem, what would you do to dramatise its meaning?

6 Explain the meaning of the following lines:
   a) 'Our rivers of sorrow sweep the ashes
      From the murdered trees into the swamp of graves' (lines 10–11)

   b) 'Now you've chosen the trunk itself' (line 13)

   c) 'Yes, you've taken my husband's shadow
      And hidden it behind the future' (lines 14–15)

   d) 'When you killed your best hand' (line 19)

GLOSSARY

Alliteration:	The repetition of consonants or vowels at the beginning of words, or of stressed syllables within words. (An example can be found in Richard Ntiru's 'rhythm of the pestle').
Allusion:	A brief reference to a person, place or event, either in history or in previous literature, which the reader is assumed to know (e.g. Yusuf O. Kassam's 'Maji Maji').
Assonance:	The repetition of identical or related vowel sounds, especially in stressed syllables, or of identical consonants with different vowels (find examples as you go through the anthology).
Atmosphere:	The mood prevailing in a literary work. It often relates to the writer's tone.
Connotation:	The associated meanings which a word in its poetic context suggests or implies; everything in addition to the specific or *denotative* meaning. (Examples can be found in the use of imagery).
Diction:	The selection of words, i.e. the 'vocabulary' used in a work of literature. (Poets are appraised according to their choice of words).
Didactic:	A work designed to demonstrate, or to present persuasively, a moral, religious or political doctrine (e.g. A. D. Amateshe's 'The Anniversary').

Empathy:	An experience in which we are so identified with a person or an object of perception, that we seem to participate in its physical sensations (e.g. in Richard S. Mabala's 'Turnboy').
Euphony:	The use of pleasant and musical diction (e.g. in Waigwa Wachira's 'Like the Sea and Its Waters').
Figurative language:	The use of metaphor and simile.
Free Verse:	Verse written without any regular metrical pattern, and usually without rhyme. This is mainly a modern verse form. (Almost all the poetry in this anthology falls in this category).
Hyperbole:	Extravagant exaggeration (find examples as you read the poems).
Imagery:	Basically, anything descriptive and evocative in poetry; anything which helps to visualize or 'realize' a scene or situation. Sometimes the word *imagery* is used in a fairly narrow sense, to signify metaphors and similes, and the various figures of speech. But often it is used to describe whatever features in a poem help us to make an imaginative response. (You will find many examples as you read the poems).
Irony:	This refers to one thing being said when the opposite is implied. This is the underlying mode of satire, comedy, and many subdivisions such as sarcasm, ridicule, mockery. (Numerous examples of this can be found in this anthology).
Lyric:	Originally, a song set to the music of the lyre (a musical instrument). Now it refers to any poem that is 'singable' (e.g. Philippa Namutebi Barlow's 'Serenade').
Metaphor:	A word or phrase, which in ordinary usage signifies one thing, is made to stand for another, e.g. the moon was like a silver coin. Metaphor is basic to most poetry and, according to some modern thinkers, it is basic to language itself.

131

Onomatopoeia:	The use of words which resemble – or enact – the sounds they describe, e.g. 'the *murmur* of bees'; 'the *hissing* of the snake'; 'the *whistling* wind' (or in David Rubadiri's 'An African Thunderstorm').
Paradox:	A statement which at first sight appears absurd or self-contradictory, but which turns out to have a serious and tenable meaning (e.g. in Richard Ntiru's 'Twin Ceremony').
Personification:	The description of an inanimate object or an abstraction as though it were alive (e.g. in Felix Mnthali's 'Farewell to a Volkswagen').
Refrain:	The repetition of a phrase, a line or a series of lines at the same point in each stanza throughout a poem (e.g. in Lillian Ingonga's 'The Dawn').
Rhetorical Questions:	Questions asked not to evoke a reply, but to achieve a stronger rhetorical emphasis than that of direct statement (e.g. in Everett Standa's 'Wedding Eve').
Sibilance:	The production of a hissing sound for poetic effect (e.g. in Theo Luzuka's 'The Motoka').
Simile:	A direct comparison between two essentially different things, introduced by the words 'like' or 'as'. (Find examples in this anthology).
Stanza:	A stanza is a division in the formal pattern of a poem, signified by a space between groups of lines. (Most of the poems in this anthology have evidence of this).
Structure:	The organization or total design of a particular poem; the 'form' to which all the parts contribute.
Style:	The characteristic manner of expression in a poem: *how* it says what it says, and is what it is. 'Style' can be analysed in terms of the various categories which this glossary lists – a poem's diction, stanza form, imagery and so on.
Symbol:	At its simplest, a 'symbol' is any word or thing taken to represent something else,

132

especially an abstract concept. So the cross is a symbol of Christianity. Words themselves are 'symbols' of ideas; they help us to convey our private and internal concepts to other minds (e.g. in David Kihazo's 'Rain').

Tone: The author's attitude to the subject matter on the one hand, and to the audience on the other, implied in the structure and style of a literary work.

Index of Poems by Author

Amateshe, A.D.
At A Zebra crossing 65
By the Seaside 122
Drowned in the Murmuring Crowd 64
Flight No. BA-067 127
Mother of Children 125
Nyalgunga 66
The Anniversary 123
Angira, Jared
Armanda 117
Braying on and on . . . 50
The letters 120
The final appeal 119
The Moslem Grave-Digger 49
Barlow, E.H.S.
Beloved 21
Barlow, Philippa Namutebi
Destiny 20
Serenade 56
Bukenya, Austin
I Met a Thief 96
Erapu, Laban
The Guilt of Giving 94
Imbuga, Francis
To the Shameless One 128
Facelift For Kafira 63
Indangasi, Henry
The Death of My Father 74
Ingonga, Lillian
Come, My Mother's Son 44
The Dawn 80
Kabuye, Kalungi
Horizons 57
The end begins: words 23
The Struggle 97
A Homecoming 19
Karamagi, Innocent
A Writer's Poem 62
Kariara, Jonathan
A Leopard Lives in a Muu Tree 110

OPENING DOORS FOR WORKING CLASS ACTORS

A Practical Guide to Entering the Industry

Patricia Jones

First published 2022

Copyright ©2022 Patricia Jones

All Rights Reserved

ISBN 9798430399382

ACKNOWLEGMENTS

With huge thanks to Andrea and Mark (Dave) Wade for the help, encouragement and advice over the months it has taken to research and write this book. Mark Jones for editing my ideas into something resembling sense. Brian Jones for keeping me together when I thought I'd lost the entire manuscript from my laptop. My friends and Mastermind group, Leanne, James, Jason, Luis, Laetitia and Mihai for whom everything is possible.

Reece Dinsdale, Jim Cartwright and Vici Wreford Sinnott for taking the time to support this idea.

CONTENTS

Introduction

An Actor's Life for Me

Where to Begin?

Training Courses

Casting Workshops

Tools of the Trade: Headshots

Getting The Best Out of Your Showreel

Showreel Companies

Casting Directories and Services

Approaching an Agent

Contacting Casting Directors

Auditions

Self-Tapes

Role Play Work

Your Mental Health and Wellbeing

Personal Safety

Final Word

Recommended Reading

Useful Organisations

INTRODUCTION

There has been a lot of discussion and press attention regarding working class actors in recent years; the difficulty accessing quality training, the prohibitive cost of travel to auditions, the lack of opportunities in general. Briefly, how much higher and tougher the mountain is to climb if you are not from a so-called 'privileged' background. It is as a response to this publicity that I decided to write this book to create an easy to follow guide of the basics you need to open doors and equip you with the tools of your craft.

To be clear from the outset, this is not intended to be a moan or to set middle and working-class actors against each other but rather, it is a practical guide based on the questions I hear frequently from aspiring actors wishing to start a career, but without the financial resources or practical knowledge to do so. My intention is to offer some, hopefully, useful advice on where to train, headshots, showreels, Spotlight membership, castings, contacting agents and casting directors as well as some tips on mindset, self-confidence and dealing with the inevitable rejection.

I have attended several of the workshops and courses mentioned in the book, so can speak from personal experience about their quality and value for money. I have also chosen to highlight several classes, photographers and showreel companies outside of London to facilitate those not in, or within easy reach of the Capital. There is always a mountain of questions regarding showreels and head shots, so I have included some tips, dos and don'ts along with links to companies who offer an excellent service at affordable prices.

The information is correct at the time of writing, and I have included links and website details of all organisations mentioned. But do double check as things can and do change and people move offices. Research is in fact a large part of an actor's work and pays huge dividends.

None of the organisations listed have paid to be part of this publication, nor am I sponsoring any of them. I have chosen them based on personal experience and research.

Good luck and keep going. Be open hearted and open minded. 'All the world's a stage' and there is most certainly a place upon it for you to play your part.

AN ACTOR'S LIFE FOR ME

To give a bit of context before we get into practical matters, it might be useful to tell you a little bit about myself, my background, and my journey through the business.

I was born in Tynemouth, near Newcastle upon Tyne. My dad was in the Navy and away from home a lot and my mum had at least three jobs, often all at the same time. I remember her working for The Provident, driving a meat delivery van for the local butcher and working in the council offices. My parents divorced when I was 16 which I mention only because it had a subsequent impact on my first steps into the industry and could have potentially ended my ambitions there and then.

As a child, I loved television and film. I loved the stories, the costumes and especially the actors. I can't say what it was about them, but I was irresistibly drawn. They held a magic and an aura that I would spend hours trying to emulate. I think I was about 5 years old when I first saw the film 'Solomon and Sheba' on television, and the weeks following saw me dressed in a pink veil 'being' Gina Lollobrigida while floating round the back garden re-enacting the scenes from the film. I put on shows in our garage and forced the other kids in the street to be in them. We performed for our parents and neighbours, acting out scenes from 'Emmerdale Farm' (as it was then) and 'Coronation Street'. As I write, I note that I have worked on both of those wonderful shows.

I clearly remember sitting at my desk at school, looking out through the thick glass doors into the long corridor and wondering how a kid like me could do THAT. How could it ever be possible for me to become an actor? I didn't come from a remotely theatrical background and up until that point had only been to the theatre once or twice to see the local pantomime at Christmas. I knew that there had to be a way and it was at that moment I made up my mind to set about finding out how.

But where to start? As a working-class kid from Newcastle growing up in the 1970s there wasn't a wealth of information to hand. I asked my mum and she reliably informed me that it was a very precarious profession and I'd always be out of work. Next stop was the careers advisor at school. He looked at my reports and said that as I had a flair for science, I would be better suited to the Milk Marketing Board! Undeterred by the former advice and unimpressed by the second, I continued to work out a strategy.

And this is where the universe intervened.

I was reading the TV Times. At the back of the magazine was a letters page, where a woman had written in to say that her daughter wanted to be an actor but didn't know where to start.

The reply informed her (and me) that The Stage newspaper was the best way to get into the business as it carried job advertisements. This was it! What I had been looking for. I raced downstairs to the kitchen and told my mum about my discovery. I must make it clear that my mum supported me in everything I did and was super proud of all my achievements, but at this point she wasn't exactly on board. 'That's just for London people' she told me 'And it'll be very expensive'. I went straight out of the house to the newsagents around the corner and asked if they had a copy of The Stage. Of course, they didn't, but were happy to order it in for me. 'How much is it?' I asked. It was 20p. 20p?!! That was nothing.

I could afford it and made my order. When it arrived, I devoured every word. I was 15.

When I was 16, I auditioned for and was accepted into Northumberland Youth Theatres. NYT was run like a professional theatre company in as much as we were expected to be prepared to work, know our lines and be on time. When the RSC was in Newcastle as part of their season, we had the opportunity to work with the wonderful Cicely Berry, voice coach of the company. I loved it. My first role was as Curio in 'Twelfth Night' which we took to Germany as part of a youth exchange programme. It was while I was with the Youth Theatre that I went on a trip to see the RSC at Newcastle Playhouse, which is now Northern Stage. Jane Lapotaire was performing as Piaf in the play of the same name written by Pam Gems. As I left the theatre and travelled home, I knew what I was going to do with the rest of my life.

I stayed with the Youth Theatre until I was 18. I left school and became a dental nurse for a year, during which time I was auditioning for drama schools in London. I was accepted at East 15 and was delighted. The next step was to get funding. Little did I know my battle had just begun.

It was the very early years of the 1980s and Student Loans had yet to be created. Educational awards were in the form of a grant which was awarded by the local authority where you lived. They were either mandatory, for subjects such as medicine and teaching, or discretionary which meant that it was necessary to meet certain criteria before being awarded one. The Arts fell into the latter category. Discretionary grants were based upon parental income, and as I was by now in a single parent family, my dad having left the previous year, I was considered in a low-income bracket. Therefore, I would need a full grant. After I made my initial application, I had to audition for The Director of Education but I was refused funding from the Education Authority on financial grounds. I wrote to my local MP who took up my case, contacted the Authority on my behalf and met with the principal of East 15, who was also fighting my corner. The local press heard about the story and this was how I found out that I had been refused again. 'GRANT BLOW TO RISING STAR', I read in the paper. So that was that. No money so no drama school. The very next day, I went into the dental surgery where I was still working as a nurse, resigned, and started to prepare my next move. I was off to London.

A friend from the Youth Theatre was about to start at Drama Centre, London, so we decided to share a flat together.

We found a studio flat near Finchley Road. My friend began his course and I started looking for work. I did some auditions for fringe shows in London pub theatres and after a while I started to get offered roles. Most of the shows weren't very good, some were terrible, one or two were excellent and gained national press attention and helped me to begin creating a CV. I would recommend everyone getting some theatre under their belts, even if it means working unpaid until you get some credits. Most profit-share companies are very flexible, will accommodate day jobs and rehearse in the evening and weekends.

I invited industry people to see my work and, eventually, secured my first agent. It was not long after that I was offered my first paid role at Leicester Haymarket (now

The Curve). I continued to work in theatre on and off but had long spells out of work, so I took jobs in call centres and did promotion work. It wasn't easy. I was always broke, lived in a variety truly horrible places and often felt despondent.

Then one day, the call came. My agent rang and said that Matthew Robinson, the Executive Producer of 'Byker Grove', the long running children's TV series wanted to see me for a regular role. The train fare to Newcastle was £60.00 return and I begged and borrowed to scrape the money together so I could go. After the first meeting, I was asked back for a screen test and then I was offered the job. My agent rang to say they wanted me to play the role of Jean Turnbull and the contract was to be for two years. In fact, it ran for four and they were among the happiest days I have ever spent. I loved that job. It gave me the television experience I needed, and I met a lot of different directors who then offered me work on subsequent shows they were working on. When I finished on 'Byker' I went back to London and did 'Eastenders' and 'Grange Hill' amongst other shows. From then on, I continued to work as an actor. I still worked day jobs in between acting work, and I still do when the situation demands, but I had done it. Against all the odds, I was an actor. I subsequently went on to work on 'Coronation Street, 'Emmerdale' 'Doctors' as well as The West End and regional theatre.

Persistence is key. It is essential. Do the work, keep your eye firmly focused on your goal and keep going.

I hope this message is clear, and I hope that you will find the following pages useful in preparing you for your career as an actor.

WHERE TO BEGIN?

Perhaps the first question you need to ask yourself is : 'why do I want to be an actor?' If the answer is 'to be famous', 'to become a celebrity' or 'get millions of Instagram followers', then I would respectfully suggest that this is not the career for you. The following pages are intended to help ease your way through the early stages of your work, but the truth is, it can be tough. You need to have passion, dedication, resilience, and total commitment to even begin to crack the surface of the profession. Reality television makes it look simple, and it is a fact that some people have risen to 'celebrity' status. However, you need to be honest and ask yourself if you are willing to take a potentially harder, longer, more difficult route that will ultimately pay greater rewards and bring so much more satisfaction and growth as an artist.

Watch other actors work. Go to the theatre. It can be pricey, but even if you go once a month you will most likely see everything you want to. Go to smaller scale venues on the fringe, too. You will learn a lot and it's a good way to make contacts. Most importantly, go to classes and learn your craft. This is essential and could make the difference between you booking a job or not. Read. Read plays, autobiographies, the history of theatre, books on the craft. Being well informed about your industry will serve you well and it all counts towards becoming a fully rounded performer. I have met several new actors who just want to work in television, but having a grounding in theatre is fundamental. You need to be able to use your voice, understand text, learn how to create a character, and maintain it over the course of a long run.

And learn to embrace Shakespeare. Forget the idea that he is just for actors with well-modulated tones and perfect RP* accents. Shakespeare is for everybody. I played Bottom in a production of 'A Midsummer Night's Dream' with a strong Geordie accent. Full disclosure: I resisted Shakespeare for a long time, then I made a conscious decision to study him. It changed my way of thinking as a performer. It taught me to look differently at how I approach a text and gave me an understanding of the importance of punctuation. I discovered how playful Shakespeare is, the incredible scope it gives the actor, and it is great fun!

All the above is, of course, just my opinion, so do with it what you will.

In the following pages we will begin to discuss the steps you will need to take. I have put them into a logical sequence so that each step will prepare you to take the next one. Some suggestions will resonate with you more than others but do keep an open mind. Be creative and prepared to try things out. If something is not for you, discard it and move on. That is part of the creative process. Be courageous!

*RP = Received Pronunciation: the standard form of British English pronunciation based on speech in Southern England and widely accepted as standard elsewhere.

TRAINING COURSES AND WORKSHOPS

Knowing where to find the right training course can be time consuming and confusing, so I have put together a selection here. With locations in Leeds, Newcastle, Manchester, Liverpool and London they offer the opportunity for quality training, while reducing some of the need to travel great distances.

All the courses are taught by professional instructors or working actors and practitioners, and they offer comprehensive training at affordable prices. I have included links to the websites of all courses mentioned, so do visit them for more details. All information is correct at the time of publication, but it is always best to check class times and prices as these things can change.

Some of the courses follow a syllabus and require regular attendance to get the most out of them, while others run as drop-in lessons and offer a degree of flexibility. Of course, like any kind of learning and training, you get out of it what you put in so be prepared to take notes and work on them in your free time between sessions.

I have included some courses that are only focused on television technique and others that offer training in craft. One or two offer both, such as The Actors Forge in Newcastle, MAP in Manchester and City Lit in London, where there are very wide selections of workshops on offer.

David Johnson Drama

David Johnson is a highly successful independent acting tutor. His studio is in the heart of Manchester, a short walk from Victoria train station and opposite the Printworks. Former students have gone on to win BAFTAs, Oliviers, Tonys, Golden Globes and an Oscar!

Classes are run on a purely practical basis via his own methods drawn from extensive experience in the business. For the adult course you need to be a minimum of 18. There is no upper age limit, so this is a great course for later entrants into the industry. Previous experience is not needed as you will be placed on the course that is right for you after meeting David for a short audition. Working professionals also attend sessions to stay on top of their game. The groups are kept small, so each student has a lot of individual attention working directly with David. This is where you will have the opportunity to perform the piece previously assigned to you which you must have prepared thoroughly. You will then receive notes and be given detailed direction into the character's motivation, emotional state and background thus creating a layered and textured performance. Be prepared to work for a few weeks on the same text to get the very best out of it and yourself.

The course follows the academic year in how terms are divided, and typically lasts two years. However, many people continue beyond that time in order to keep their skill set honed. The course is designed to maximise your potential as an actor in all mediums, so as well as the modules described below, you will also do camera work and learn the skills required for television. Scenes are filmed with state-of-the-art cameras then played back to you for technical and creative feedback. Sessions run once a fortnight and last a minimum of 2.5 hours. You will be active and working for the entire session.

The Adult Courses are divided into modules which include:

Script Analysis

You will study a monologue for character, location, physical and emotional aspects and then move on to work on duologues which explore reaction and develop essential listening skills. Typically, you will study your monologue or duologue for a few sessions, uncovering a deeper understanding of textual context and meaning.

Emotional Bias

In these sessions you are encouraged to delve deeper into the emotional life of a character. How did they get where they are? What is their backstory? David teaches how to BE rather than act and the emphasis is very much on simplicity and honesty. Using David's system, you will begin to access deeper and more truthful performances and create authentic, believable characters.

Character

In this module you will study body awareness, physical observation and implementation. In other words, how your character moves and what influences and informs their movement. Location? Age? Emotion? You will also spend time studying animals which is great fun and can be incredibly useful when creating a character. It is also very freeing as you are encouraged to let go of your own physicality and create something completely new.

Textual Coordination

Moving into the more advanced aspects of text you will study classical and modern works including Shakespeare. You will develop a profound understanding of language and why a playwright chooses the words they do. Detailed study of nuance and subtext add another layer of texture to your work making your performance more compelling.

During the course there are various showcases where agents and casting directors are invited to see the work you have been doing throughout the year and where you can demonstrate your talent and skill.

These classes are like going to drama school in their depth and precision. David is very detailed in his work, and you will be required to arrive at each session fully prepared and ready to work. Be prepared to learn how to think like an actor and to be able to discuss text and imagery, giving your reasons why.

And don't be late!! David also teaches theatrical etiquette and good time- keeping for an actor is essential. You can't arrive at the theatre late for your half-hour call. Nor can you be late for David's classes. Begin the way you mean to go on and be professional in your attitude, preparation and behaviour.

David Johnson Drama also runs classes for young people and children, and you can find information of these on the website.

https://www.djohnsondrama.com

2nd Floor, Pleer House, 1 Fennel Street, Manchester M4 3DU Tel: 07969 183481

Class duration 2.5 hours

Email: johnsondrama@googlemail.com

Cost: Sessions are ongoing and cost £22.50 per session payable in a two-session block of £45.00

ActUpNorth

Founded in 2009 by Peter Hunt CDG, now Head of Casting for Lime Pictures UK and Casting Director of Hollyoaks, ActUpNorth has grown to be one of the largest and most successful independent training schools outside of London with bases in Manchester, Leeds and Liverpool.

The school offers a unique syllabus taught by highly skilled industry professionals and working actors. The course and additional masterclasses are designed to fully prepare both new and established performers alike for the realities of working professionally in the industry.

Actors attend a one 2-hour workshop each week, where they gain invaluable guidance from invited guest tutors and industry practitioners. These include casting directors, producers, directors and agents.

In 2020, ActUpNorth began offering online classes to facilitate the need to adapt their methods of training during the pandemic. The online offering has proved so popular, that the online work continues and has opened the classes nationally and internationally, with students now joining from as far afield as Australia and the USA.

Their unique techniques and methods are designed to equip actors with a complete skill set for the modern industry. Entry to the classes is via an initial group audition which is both friendly and fun. If successful in gaining a place, students are monitored and observed throughout, so progress is clear and measurable. Feedback is given during and at the end of every lesson to give the student the personal guidance they need to develop and progress in their work. Specific notes are given, which the student then puts into action, aiding immediate understanding of the techniques and, ultimately, the process of creating a character while working within the technical demands of television and film.

Classes mainly concentrate on 'Acting for Camera', but the 'Acting Technique' classes can be applied and adapted to suit a range of mediums.

Students work on scripts from current and past TV series and are given time to prepare the scene. Detailed and bespoke advice is given on how to understand and 'break down' a script and, once prepared, students perform their scene with a partner which is filmed. Scenes are then played back for constructive and supportive feedback.

ActUpNorth continues to evolve their approach to stay relevant in an everchanging climate. A 'term' typically lasts for 12 to 16 weeks and is divided into three modules, each lasting for approximately 3 weeks. This means that students can join the classes at various points during the year. Consistent attendance every week is recommended to gain the best results. Classes run for 2 hours. Details of term dates can be found by visiting the ActUpNorth website via the link, below.

Work included in the course includes: 'Acting and Casting for TV Drama and Commercials', 'Character Development', 'Acting for TV vs Film / Stage', 'Acting for Period Drama', 'Acting for Soaps', 'Technicalities of Screen Acting', 'Finding an Agent' and 'The Life of an Actor'. The minimum commitment to study with ActUpNorth is one term.

Students have gone on to work in various high profile TV dramas, soaps, films, TV ad campaigns for global brands and theatre work at the likes of 'The National Theatre', and 'The Royal Exchange', to name but two.

Fees: Classes are priced at £18 for two hours. This includes the cost of all additional visiting tutor classes. A fee of £72 is payable in advance for four weeks and discounts are available for those wishing to pay for the entire term in advance.

https://actupnorth.com/

Email: info@actupnorth.com

Tel: 0844 8111740

Locations:

Manchester: 4th Floor, Unit G, 8 Lower Ormond Street, Manchester M1 5QF

Leeds: Studio 71, 71 Kirkstall Road, Leeds LS3 1LH

Liverpool: Suite 325, 3rd Floor, QD Business Centre, Norfolk St, Liverpool L1 0BG

The Actors Forge

The Actors Forge, founded in 2018 by Daniel Matthew Lemon, is a collective of actors, writers and producers based in and around Newcastle and the Northeast of England. Its mission is to develop a community of actors and creatives dedicated to learning about the craft of acting and improving access to professional work. They offer weekly classes and workshops with some of the industry's leading professionals. It is open to all levels and there are currently two courses running: an Advanced course for actors who are represented or are active in the industry and a Foundation course for those looking to learn the craft and business of acting. Courses take place on Wednesday and Thursday evenings from 6.00-9.00pm. There are also semi-regular stage combat courses and details of when these will be happening can be found on the website. The emphasis of each course is to work with the pace of the individual actor and offer a pathway for development into the industry.

Classes take place at St John the Baptist Church in central Newcastle and typically begin with a physical and vocal warm up. Good vocal technique is an essential requirement for your actor's toolbox, so this is an excellent opportunity to practise and learn new techniques. Acting methodologies such as Meisner and Stanislavski are taught to encourage and explore emotional realism, authenticity in your work and character analysis. Students can explore different methods to find which one resonates the most. The Actors Forge also offers Masterclasses led by some of the country's leading casting directors, directors and agents. Previous tutors include, Peter Hunt, Head of Casting at Hollyoaks, Andrea Clark (Dog Soldiers and Blade II), Faye Timby (The Witcher), Claire Bleasdale and Anita Gilbert, Head of Voice at Speak Easy Voices who offer voice and accent coaching. Feedback and advice offered during all sessions is tailored to each individual actor. Workshops also run online so you don't have to travel to Newcastle to get the benefit of directors such as Ruth Carney (Emmerdale, Casualty, Death in Paradise) and Steve Hughes (Casualty, Miss Scarlet and the Duke).

The Actors Forge does not operate like a traditional drama school. Rather, it is a place to meet, work and network with other creatives. Advice is given on practical aspects of the industry such as how to build credits in order to get your Spotlight entry, how to successfully audition and how to approach an agent. Head over to the Actors Forge website to see showreels and CVs of actors who have trained with them. It will give you a great overview of the work. There is also a resource page for finding a monologue which suits you which you can use to practise and for auditions if requested (they aren't always, these days). Actors Forge has a partnership with RGR Film Productions who produce monologue and scene reels, voice reels and headshots. Prices for these are available upon request, via the website.

The location for the courses has good disabled access with a small lip into the main entrance of the building which also has a wheelchair-accessible toilet.

Cost of classes and workshops: Advanced and Foundation courses £165 for an 8-week term. There are 5 terms a year.

Masterclasses: £40-£60 and usually take place on a Saturday.

https://theactorsforge.com/

dan@theactorsforge.com

St John the Baptist Church, Grainger Street,

Newcastle NE1 5JG

Tel: 0771 6946100

act4tv

As the name suggests, act4tv is fully focused on the training and teaching of technique and competencies for television performance. There is a world of difference between acting for the stage, film and television. TV work requires an understanding of how to pitch a performance for drama, comedy and soap, each requiring their own knowledge and skill set.

The act4tv group was founded in 2009 by casting director Michael Jackson who is prolific in the casting of dramas such as Ackley Bridge, Time, Help and Happy Valley. His mission is to create a training ground that prepares actors in what is expected of them and how best to succeed in the audition room. An actor's audition is often an indication of how they might be on set, so there is no room for being unprepared or uncertain of your job.

Tutors are all working actors with impressive credits, including Ackley Bridge, Line of Duty, Coronation Street and All Creatures Great and Small. Full biographies can be found on the act4tv website, details listed below.

Studio classes are held in Manchester, Leeds and Liverpool and there are also online courses available. Minimum age for adult classes is 18 but they do run courses for younger performers every Sunday in all three studios. Act4tv prepares students for the AUDITION in TV and film. Courses are designed so that actors are always engaged and are performing or preparing scenes for the whole session. They explore the various elements of the casting process such as delivering idents, cold readings, getting the most from a script in the 15 minutes you are in the room, breaking down and understanding the subtext of a scene and improvisation technique. All scenes are recorded and reviewed in class so that constructive feedback can be given. Students can also review their own work at home, which is an invaluable resource for developing and learning from mistakes as well as great takes. Students in all three centres work on the same scripts and scenes each week, so if you can't make it to your usual location then you can jump into another class and continue from where you left off. For term dates and online booking, visit the website.

Online courses follow the same structure with students attending from all over the UK and other parts of the world.

The Actors' Hub.

This is where act4tv offers complimentary online courses with high profile industry professionals. Events take place a couple of times a month and are exclusive to members. Places are limited and demand is high, so students need to apply to be considered. Previous guests include casting director Dan Hubbard and actor Gurjeet Singh. Keep up to date with events and news by signing up to the mailing list and follow on social media.

Scholarships for children will be on offer in 2022

https://act4.tv/adults/

Email: hello@act4tv

Cartwright Drama Studio

Founded by the celebrated and award-winning playwright, screenwriter and director, Jim Cartwright, The Cartwright Drama Studio was set up to help actors gain access to training and entry into the industry. The aim of the studio is to develop as a space for exploration and experimentation, while equipping performers with the necessary skills needed to enter the profession. Adult classes run in Manchester and Chorley with good transport links to both. Entry is by application only and you can apply via the website, details of which are listed overleaf. Classes are taught by Jim himself who has a unique way of working based on his own experience. Students are encouraged to begin with the imagination, where all creativity begins and from where the classes grow and develop, incorporating script and audition work, film and TV acting. Students are actively supported and guided to write their own work which they develop to performance at one of the showcases offered as part of the syllabus.

Courses are comprehensive and cover full training in stage, film and television. They are open to students with no prior experience in acting as well as working professional actors who want to keep their skills up to date. There is no upper age limit and Jim has students who are taking their first steps into the business in their 70s so don't be deterred by age!

Masterclasses with renowned industry professionals such as Maxine Peake and Jane Horrocks support and guide students on how to work professionally and develop as artists. There are regular performance opportunities at the Cartwright Palladium and showcases where you can invite agents and casting directors to see your work.

Alongside the studio, members will have the opportunity of representation as an associate of Cartwright Higgins Agency where you will be submitted for professional work should the right role come along. The agency was set up by Jim Cartwright and Tracy Higgins with the aim of offering a fresh approach to representing talent. Clients have successfully secured bookings on Coronation Street, The Bay, Brassic, Netflix Dramas and Number One Theatre tours. After you have been a member of the Studio for a period of one month, you can, if you choose, to become a member of CHAS and an associate of Cartwright Higgins Management. Whilst this does not entitle you to all the benefits of being a full member of the agency, it does give you the opportunity to be considered for professional roles in film, TV and theatre. There are some stipulations to adhere to and they are as follows:

You must have attended Cartwright Drama Studio for a period of at least one month.

You must be prepared to supply professional head shots.

You must join Casting Networks which is free to members. You can also join as a non-member, as a paid service.

You must be prepared to travel to London for some castings. (You would only be submitted for London castings if the work was financially viable, and you indicated you would be happy to travel for the role in question). Membership to CHAS is only valid for existing students and will be stopped if and when you leave the course. If the agency secures work for you, you will be charged the standard rates which are 10% for theatre and 15% for television and commercials.

The Jim Cartwright Company is a professional theatre company resident at the multi -million-pound Adelphi Theatre in Salford.

Adult Acting Classes: email cartwrightdramastudio@gmail.com

Tel:01257 264641

Chorley: Cartwright Drama Studio, Primrose Bank House, Friday Street, PR6 0AA

Manchester: 72 Tib Street, Northern Quarter, Manchester M4 1LG

Salford (Media City) New Adelphi Theatre, Orange Tower, Salford Quays, M50 2HE

Website: https://www.cartwrightdramastudio.co.uk

Manchester Actors Platform (MAP)

Created in 2015 by actor / acting coach Simon Naylor, MAP was designed to help adult actors in their training and provide professional services at affordable prices, including headshots and help with self-tapes. As MAP offers a complete service to actors, I have divided each of these into sections for easy referral.

Classes

Classes can be workshops, weekend courses and / or 6–8-weeks blocks and focus on a specific discipline such as scene study, improvisation, voice, Shakespeare, scriptwriting and movement. Various practitioners visit and work with students to develop their skills in each area. Classes are to be booked in advance and can paid be for over a period of weeks before the lessons begin. (Prices at the time of publication are correct but please check the MAP website for any changes). Classes mirror those you might find on a three-year acting course and reflect the rigours of such a course, so paying in advance is a great incentive to keep you motivated and engaged.

Screen Acting

Courses take place over a period of 8 weeks, one evening a week for 4 hours (usually 5.30-9.30). Classes are kept small to ensure the work is detailed, focused and intense. There are three terms and they are progressive so one term must be completed before moving on to the next. This ensures a thorough and logical sequence to learning, with measurable progress throughout the entirety of the course. Sessions focus on all the essentials needed to create a truthful and real performance such as active listening, being in the moment and NOT acting! Technical notes are also studied for example, hitting your mark and the TV voice. The first three terms are made up of the Entry class and then move on to Advanced and Professional classes. All terms must be completed before moving on to the next to ensure a complete, rounded training.

Cost: £350 for all 8 weeks (Payment must be made before the start of the first class).

A £100 deposit is required by all students to secure a place on the course. Payments can be made at the time of registration and include VAT.

Where: 53two studios,

Great Northern Warehouse, Unit 2, 235 Deansgate, Manchester M3 4EN.

Shakespeare Sorted

If the idea of performing Shakespeare has always filled you with fear, you are not alone. It is only in recent years that I have begun to embrace the joy of his work and understand the freedom it gives an actor to create. MAP runs 90-minute workshops over 4 weeks to develop your confidence and free your performance. Sessions involve work on iambic pentameter and the rhythms and how to use them, by using a selection of script extracts from some of Shakespeare's most famous texts. You will have time to learn and prepare a two-minute monologue which you will then work on in the group and receive constructive, supportive feedback.

Cost: £120 for 4 weeks (payment must be made before the beginning of the first class)

A £30 deposit is required by all students to secure a place on the course and can be paid at the time of registration.

Please check out the website for current days and times of the classes.

Where: 53two Studios

Scene Study

This course takes place over 6 weeks and is designed to allow actors to focus on a contemporary script from day one of rehearsals to performance level. Working in intense detail, the sessions will explore the history of the play, the world in which it is set and how that world affects the characters. The aim of the course is to give actors a greater understanding of how to work on theatre and television scripts and how to develop and cement their own process. The course mirrors the training at established UK drama schools across the country and provides an individual training for each actor. Where possible, the class work is in pairs, so commitment is essential to fully get the benefits of the sessions.

Cost: £200pp (a non-refundable deposit of £60 is payable at the point of registration to confirm your place). Please check the MAP website for current dates and times of the classes.

Where: 53two Studios.

Online Classes

These are perfect if you are not able to get to Manchester or your schedule doesn't support the live classes. Sessions are practical and can be used to perfect some skills, ask questions and learn the requisite techniques for TV and theatre. MAP is also now offering singing lessons available to all levels in the comfort of your own home.

Below is a list of online classes MAP regularly run. There is a choice of 1:1 and group sessions.

Group Workshops

Acting Process Perfected (3 Sessions) £50

Shakespeare Sorted (3 Sessions) £50

Connection - What is It? (2 Sessions) £30

The Perfect Self Tape (4 Sessions) £120

1:1 Sessions

Monologue Work (around your schedule in 1-hour sessions) £60

Actors' MOT (Around your schedule) £10

Singing and Acting

Acting through Song (Around your Schedule) £20

Further detailed description of these classes can be found at the MAP website along with instant booking access.

53two and Manchester Actor's Platform pride themselves on ensuring that accessibility is at the heart of what they do. As such, the theatre and studio are fully accessible to ensure that people with disabilities can attend shows / workshops etc. The modular table system, lowered bar and adaptable staging mean that wheelchair users can use all elements of the venue. All shows produced by 53two have at least one BSL performance (depending on run length) and visiting companies are offered subsidised rates to also provide a BSL performance. Bar staff are trained to converse in BSL, forging strong links with the Manchester Deaf Centre. For neuro-divergent patrons and/or creatives, ear-defenders and/or 'chill out' zones are available when required. 53two works with Triple C, a charity supporting disabled creatives,

https:www.maplatform.co.uk/

City Lit London

Located in the heart of London's West End, City Lit is one of the oldest and best-established educational facilities in London. It is a state funded adult education centre offering full and part-time acting and theatre courses for all adults, whatever their background, age and aspiration. Including acting, musical theatre, stage combat, comedy, professional and physical skills for actors. Tutors come from professional backgrounds and training is practical, creative and supportive. Examples of classes are listed below but are not exhaustive, so do check out the website for full details, dates and times. City Lit is a huge organisation with a wealth of courses in a variety of creative disciplines too many to mention here. However, I have chosen a selection to give you an idea of what is on offer. There are also details of sessions held online. Courses are taught by industry professionals and working actors and generally take place in the evening and weekends, so are perfect if you are working. Prices for the courses vary and there are reductions for senior students as well as concessions for low-income and unwaged. Check out the Fees and Finance information in the Help area for details on how to pay for your course, what support is available and childcare facilities and access.

Improvisation Workshop

Designed to develop and enrich your skills as an actor through improvisation, this is a safe and supportive environment in which to explore your creativity, make mistakes to have fun. You will learn the key techniques required to perform effective improvisational work. The sessions are in the classroom and are held in the evenings.

Play reading

Get together with other actors to explore the work of different playwrights. These are online sessions and are designed for those who wish to develop an understanding of the main themes in a selection of classical and modern texts, developing your knowledge of writing styles and how to get the most from a text.

Acting Shakespeare

Rehearse and perform scenes and speeches from Shakespeare's plays. This is a class suitable for all levels including those new to Shakespeare. You will develop the ability to create vivid performances that are both true to life and true to the language. This course takes place in the classroom.

Acting for Fun

This is a class for complete beginners where you can learn to play, explore and be brave through acting exercises and games. Relax and let your creativity run wild.

City Lit Theatre Company

A wonderful opportunity to be part of a theatre company, working alongside technical students and those training on the directors' courses to create a play from scratch in just 6 weeks! The course takes place in the evenings and the full rehearsal schedule is on available online. This should be checked before booking to make sure you are able to attend all the sessions.

If you are considering auditioning for drama school, City Lit offers an Accredited Acting Course. There are currently two part-time accredited options – Foundation (a Level 2 Extended Certificate) and Acting Diploma (Level 3). Both are accredited by Open College Network, London. The courses are perfect if you are working as you can fit them in around your schedule. For further details contact audition@citylit.ac.uk.

https://www.citylit.ac.uk/courses/performing-arts/acting-and-theatre

Address: 1-10 Keely Street, London WC2B 4BA

Tel: 020 7831 7831

Email: infoline@citylit.ac.uk

Accessibility at Keely Street includes disabled parking, step free access, toilets and changing facilities. There is a short video on the website showing all facilities available.

Open Door

Open Door is an organisation that helps talented young people who do not have the financial support or resources to gain a place at one of the UK's leading drama schools.

Students will complete an 8-month intensive course designed to give actors what they need to take the next steps in their career. Courses are open to people between the ages of 18-26 (acting) and 17-26 (behind the scenes training). They work from bases in London, Essex, Rotherham and East Midlands. The aim is to help students through some of the potential obstacles and to equip them with the skill set they need to feel confident and prepared in auditions – AND IT'S ALL FREE!!!

Successful acting applicants will receive:

Six free auditions at UK leading drama schools including RADA, LAMDA Guildhall, Royal Welsh College of Music and Drama, Royal Central School of Speech and Drama and The Royal Conservatoire of Scotland.

Free travel to any drama school audition outside of your area.

15 hours of 1:1 acting tutoring from experienced industry professionals.

Musical tutoring for any musical auditions

Bespoke workshops led by industry professionals

Free theatre trips

Bursary and funding advice.

To be eligible to apply for the acting bursary you must be based in London, Essex, Sheffield, Rotherham or East

Midlands. You must also have an annual family income of £30,000 or less, be aged between 18-26 (you must be 18 by 1st September 2022), not currently have a degree, have a commitment to acting as your career, intend to apply for a full time BA Honours degree in acting for the 21/22 academic year and be a UK citizen, or have lived in the UK long enough to be eligible for UK student finance.

Applications will open in July 2022, and you can apply directly from the Open Door website.

Website: https://www.opendoor.org.uk/

Address: Open Door People,

Studio 9, 6 Cliff Road, London NW1 9AN
email:info@opendoor.org.uk

YAFTA International

Yorkshire Academy of Film and Television Acting

YAFTA offers weekly classes and workshops in Harrogate, Leeds, Sheffield and York. Its aims are to prepare all students for work as professional television and film actors and to equip them with the necessary skills, tools, knowledge and psychological preparation required to succeed in the film and TV industry. Students are encouraged to be professional, punctual, polite and reliable throughout their training with YAFTA and beyond. Classes develop team-working skills, confidence building and interpersonal relationships, all while embracing creativity.

Specialised workshops include: Auditioning for small roles on TV, acting workshops with actor and director Reece Dinsdale (Moving On and Emmerdale), directors Ian Bevitt (Emmerdale and Coronation Street) and Mickey Jones (Emmerdale, Hollyoaks, Eastenders), all of whom offer an invaluable and authentic view of how the industry works in general and what to expect when you audition and then book the job. Casting Director workshops are held on a regular basis with Faye Styring (Emmerdale), Joanne Moss (Coronation Street), Nick Laxton (Hollyoaks, Disney, Nickelodeon) and Jane Anderson (CBBC Wolfblood). Additionally, as part of the programme, students undertake training on several topics such as audition technique, how to market yourself as an actor, understanding the industry and the psychological demands it can make.

The YAFTA Acting for Screen Diploma is an 18-month blended learning course for those with little or no experience in front of the camera, and who wish to undertake extensive training, taking you from beginner to professional screen actor. Students have the opportunity of working with television directors. The course follows a structured syllabus which has been designed by graduates from leading drama schools such as RADA, LAMDA, Central School of Speech and Drama, ALRA and LIPA. This course is accredited by Spotlight which means that on completion, students are eligible to join. Courses begin in February, May and October each year and the application form can be found on the website (details listed below).

How to Start your Career as a Professional Actor in the UK and Personal Mentoring Programme.

This course runs for 15 weeks and is designed for actors who have already completed some training. It is interactive with no more than 15 students who will be required to fully engage in the weekly activities. In addition to the weekly lectures, each student will have individual mentoring sessions with Charlotte Armitage, award winning entrepreneur, talent agent and media psychologist. She will be offering individualised guidance throughout the programme to help you understand yourself, who you are as a performer and how to land your first TV role. Topics covered in the course include: an overview of the industry, creating your own personal brand, marketing tools and how to use them effectively, using social media to enhance your career and how to manage the potential pressures it may involve, representation and how to find an agent, showreels and headshots, the audition process, how to deliver a great self-tape, mental health and goal setting.

YAFTA Pro

YAFTA offers a selection of services such as headshot sessions (£120 inc. VAT) for 5 retouched images in colour and black and white.

Showreels. Three scenes are written specifically for you with locations, filming and sound recording fully edited. Showreel days can be booked, dates of which can be found on the website.

Talent Agency, representing artists of all ages for screen acting work including film, drama, soap, commercials and corporate projects. The agency not only accepts students of YAFTA but also professional actors external to the Academy. For information and to apply, email agency@yafta.co.uk. Be aware, however, that it very unlikely you will be offered representation without Spotlight, CV, headshots and a showreel so make sure you are fully equipped to make a serious and well thought-out application.

Bookings for all classes and workshops can be made through the YAFTA website. As the prices of the courses vary and there are many to choose from, I have not listed prices. However, drop-in classes cost £20 per session.

Website: https://www.yafta.co.uk/

NOTES

CASTING WORKSHOPS

There are casting workshops all over the country where you can continue your professional development and work directly with casting directors. You are normally sent a scene,(or sides), to prepare fully just as you would for a normal casting. You will then perform them and be filmed for feedback and notes. Some workshops are held on a one-to-one basis and others in small groups. They are an excellent way to practise in front of the camera, develop your technique and learn how to deal with those pesky nerves. But be aware that they are NOT auditions or opportunities to be offered work. There is generally time for Q&A at the end of the session which are useful for finding out about how a particular casting director works, likes to be contacted etc. So, make notes to refer to later.

The Actors' Guild of Great Britain

Founded by a group of professional actors, TAG is the largest membership organisation offering ongoing professional development for actors in the UK. It is run strictly for professional performers who must be over 18, registered with Spotlight, have at least 4 verifiable acting credits or have graduated from an accredited Drama School. Applicants are assessed on their individual merit. Their hub is run from the Spotlight offices in London, and they also offer workshops in the Northwest and Southeast. The workshops, seminars and masterclasses are held by industry professionals who offer an enormous wealth of experience gained during their careers. Examples of workshops available are: Casting for the screen and self-tapes, mastering an American accent, casting for comedy, casting for continuing drama and audition scenes. There are also advice sessions on how to make the best of your CV. Some of the sessions are online and you can check these out by looking at the resources section of the website. Also, in the resources section is a directory of services such as accountants, showreels, headshots, and non-acting jobs. A useful discount section is included here, where you can find money off casting websites and accountancy, once you have joined and become a member.

There are 2 types of membership available – a basic membership for £12 per year which provides you with access to discounts only and the premium membership for £24 per year, which gives access to workshops as well as the other services. (If you renew before your membership expires it costs £20). You will then pay for the workshop in which you wish to take part, in addition to the annual membership fee. These vary in price depending on the duration of the course and prices start from around £24. Full details of all current workshops can be found on the website. They are regularly updated and added to so keep checking in so you don't miss out on anything.

Website: https://www.actorsguild.co.uk/

Email: mail@actorsguild.co.uk

First Take Workshops

Set up by actress and stand-up comedian Andrea Watson in 2017, First Take Workshops were created to offer ongoing development for actors at all stages of their careers. Workshops are led by working TV directors and actors such as Ian Bevitt (Emmerdale, Coronation Street), Rick Laxton (casting director for BBC ITV and Channel 4) and actor and director Reece Dinsdale (Emmerdale, Moving On) Workshops are relatively small so you get the opportunity to work fully with the course leader and receive feedback on your performance. The environment is friendly, relaxed and fun. Also on offer are one-to-one career advice sessions, comedy bootcamp weekends and a soon-to-begin writers' workshop with Rick Laxton, for those of you who are interested in writing for the screen. Prices for the workshops vary but an acting class typically is around £50 for a morning, or an afternoon session Current workshops and pricing can be found on the website. All classes must be paid for at the time of booking. Locations for classes are in York and North Yorkshire.

Website https://www.firsttakeworkshops.co.uk/

Ben Cogan

Ben Cogan is a freelance casting director with over twenty years' experience, casting a powerhouse of award-winning dramas for film and television. After fifteen years working at the BBC, Ben created BeCo.Me in 2015 and, since then, has been involved in casting independent films and children's television as well as casting the additional child roles in 'His Dark Materials'.

Ben has a passion for working with actors and aiding them in their preparation for auditions. His sessions are relaxed and informal, at the same time as being detailed and explorative, giving the actor the opportunity to try a scene in different ways in order to discover what works best and get the best out of the performance. He will redirect the scene offering advice on how to take a note and act on it.

Classes are open to actors of all levels and ages. His studio is situated in London's Marylebone, close to transport links.

Who are the sessions for?

Graduates wanting to make a positive first impression.

Actors who are seeking pre-audition tuition.

Regularly auditioning actors who need a little help to land the role.

Actors preparing to audition for a regular role.

Actors who are returning to the industry after a career break.

Actors who predominately work in theatre but are looking to do more screen work.

Experienced actors who are anxious about auditioning.

All other actors.

Ben also takes 1:1 sessions and hosts casting workshops.

If you wish to contact BeCo.Me about being cast in a forthcoming project, please follow these guidelines.

When sending headshots and showreels, do not send excessively large files as they will not be opened. Best to send in PDF / Word Document format. If you are a member of Spotlight, just add your link to the bottom of the cover letter. If you are in a show either on stage or TV, you can invite Ben and if he is available, he will attend. Please give plenty of notice for invites. The best way to contact Ben is via email. NO telephone calls please.

Website: http://www.becometalent.com/home.html

Email: beco.me@mail.com

The Carney Academy

Ruth Carney is a TV and theatre director who has worked in the West End and on Broadway. Recent TV credits include Casualty, Father Brown, Emmerdale and Death in Paradise.

Ruth set up the Carney Academy in 2010 with the clear objective of providing industry standard performance training that unlocks the skills necessary for today's industry. Over the years, the academy has gone from strength to strength and has schools in Sheffield and Cheshire.

The Carney Studio 2022

The Carney Studio is a brand-new evolution of the Carney Academy which offers a programme of entry level, intermediate and advanced coaching and masterclasses for adults. It aims to offer a fresh new perspective for TV, film and theatre professionals to develop their skills. Classes are led by teaching faculty members and guest tutors both in group and 1:1 sessions. Masterclasses are held with experienced actors, writers, producers and other industry veterans who share a wealth of knowledge and experience. Available to students aged 16 and over, the masterclasses cover topics such as acting for camera, television audition technique, singing for wellbeing, showtunes masterclass and script and screenwriting for beginners.

For prices and dates of current workshops, contact

Website: https://www.carneyacademy.co.uk/carney-studio-adults

NOTES

TOOLS OF THE TRADE

Headshots

So, you have chosen the school where you want to train and are now developing the acting technique you need to do the job. What's next? Remember that being an actor is a job and like all jobs you will need the tools of the trade in order to work. The basics required at the beginning are a great headshot and showreel. Many actors have voice demo reels too, but I would suggest you focus on the first two as you simply can't start without them.

Let's begin with the headshot. It is your business card, your logo or your brand and it's the very first thing an agent or casting director will look at. When they are looking through Spotlight submissions, for example, your photo will be just a thumbnail, so it needs to stand out from the rest, and it must look like YOU.

What does that mean exactly? It means that it must be a superior quality, professional shot. Don't be tempted to try and save money by getting a relative or friend to take a photo. Actors' headshots are specific, and you need a reputable, professional photographer. They will talk to you about the roles you see yourself playing, your choice of clothes for the shoot and will give you advice on how to stand, your thoughts, attitude etc. Some will shoot in a studio with studio lights while others will use natural light. You can also ask for a mixture of the two. Natural light is favourable, but obviously can depend upon weather conditions.

Never be swayed by cost. Of course, we all have a budget but the most expensive is not necessarily the best for you. Always look at the work of each photographer that you are interested in before you look at the price. Make a list of your favourites and then chose one that fits your budget. I have listed some excellent and reasonably priced photographers here, but do look around at others before making a decision.

You need to know who you are, the types of roles you could realistically play and your playing age. (Not your actual age but the range you could play). If you are at a training school, you will be guided through some of this, but you must know your unique selling point, your USP. You need to know your 'type'. Are you a nurse, lawyer, criminal, hard man / woman, a mum? Think of the status of the characters and use it during the shoot. A beautiful photograph is NOT what a headshot is about. Always ask professional advice when you are choosing your shots. No friends, relatives or asking on Facebook. Ask your agent if you have one, your teacher, or contact Spotlight. A good headshot can hugely increase your chances of getting in the room, and, if they are not up to standard, you may be passed over.

Once you have thought about the roles you want to play, you can choose the right outfits for the day. Take a few choices, maybe a couple for each character, (no need for a giant suitcase full of clothes) the photographer will advise you on which work best. Female actors beware of strappy or low-cut tops. They show too much flesh and if your hair falls over the straps it can look like you aren't wearing anything. Men, if you want to show some facial hair, feel free to do so in the earlier shots, you can remove it later in the shoot for some clean-shaven choices. Never worry about spots, blemishes, eye-bags etc. Once your photos are retouched you will never know they were there, and they aren't worth cancelling a session over. That said, get a good night's sleep before your shoot day, hydrate well, and don't go drinking the night before!

During the session, you will be able to see the shots in the camera. Listen to any advice the photographer gives at this point. It will help you make any necessary adjustments and to choose your final images.

All you need to do then is to relax and enjoy the session. Think about the character you are portraying, and the camera will pick it up in your eyes. Be active. You need to engage whoever is looking at the picture; they want to see character, thoughts and energy. Headshot sessions should be fun so make sure you are fully prepared before you go, so that you can get on with showing the very best of who you are and who you can be.

The following is a list of quality professional photographers with reasonable rates, many of whom I have used myself. Remember to look at their portfolios of work to see which ones you like most. Ask for advice before, during and after your shoot to help you get the very best out of your headshots. They are worth every penny and can get you into the room. If you are still in any doubt, Spotlight runs an excellent advice service: https://www.spotlight.com/

Neilson Reeves Photography

Colin Boulter. Actor Head Shots, Manchester

Natural or studio light, theatrical and commercial headshots for actors and presenters. Colin offers 3 packages and price offers as follows.

Heading Out.

A 2-hour session with 2 set or location changes, 2 finished and retouched images. £250. There is also a media, makeup and styling option for an additional £125.

Get Ahead.

A 4-hour session with 4 set or location changes, 4 finished and retouched images. Media, makeup and styling option £150.

Heads Above.

A 5-hour session with 5 set or location changes, 4 finished and retouched images plus body shot. Media, makeup and styling included. £575.

For all packages, the beginning of the session is spent looking at clothing and a shoot plan. You will be able to chat to Colin prior to your session when you can discuss your career to date, your casting goals, and the reasons for your new headshots. If you choose the hair and makeup option, you will be advised on how to prepare your skin before the session. Colin recommends that customers choose some images from the site that they like so as get an idea of preference for natural or studio lighting. After the shoot, all images will be sent to you via a secure online proofing gallery which can be shared with agents and anyone else you may want to help you select your final pictures. There is also an option to buy additional images if you wish. Once you have chosen your photos, they will be retouched and uploaded to the studio's internet cloud and from where you can download them in different file sizes for easy emailing and sharing online.

Website: https://www.neilsonreeves.co.uk/

Studio Address

7 Egerton Road South, Manchester M21 0YP

Free parking available.

Email: Colin1boulter@gmail.com

Tel: 07935 926494

Tony Blake Photography

Chester based photographer Tony Blake has a wealth of experience collaborating with actors on set as well as in the studio. In addition to being an actors' headshot photographer, Tony works as a unit stills photographer on television productions commissioned by ITV, BBC, Channel 4 and Sky.

Tony favours a natural style while shooting. You can alter your hair and makeup during the shoot and bring a collection of clothing to change into. There is a lovely dressing room space in which to get ready. After the shoot, you will receive your high-resolution digital headshot images to choose from and Tony provides a swift service. Once you have emailed your choices, typical delivery time of the finished product is normally 10 working days, although this can vary depending on workload.

Price for an actors' headshot session £180, consultation and shoot time approx. 2 hours, digital set of contact sheets, 3 high resolution jpeg images, retouched. (Black and white can be provided at no extra cost).

To book a session, get in touch with Tony to organise times and dates.

Website:

http://www.tonyblakephoto.co.uk/northwest-actor-headshot-photographer

Studio Address: 68 Watergate Street, Chester CH1 2LA.

Email: tony@tonyblakephoto.co.uk

David John Headshots

David is a Manchester based photographer specialising in actors' headshots. Sessions are relaxed, informal, natural light and aimed at capturing the real you, so that you connect with your target audience. David also has a background in acting which helps him understand your specific needs as well as what an agent and casting director might require. He is also registered as a Spotlight photographer. The studio is located 5 minutes from Manchester Piccadilly. He also has a second location in London, 2 minutes from Angel tube station. A discounted rate for students and under 18s is available.

Before your session, David suggests that you think about what you want your headshots to say about you and the roles you are going up for. If you have agent, do they have a brief for the shoot?

A session will normally take about 90 minutes to 2 hours with student sessions lasting approximately 1 hour. You will be able to review the shots during the session and afterwards you will receive an email link (usually within 24 hours). You can make a shortlist from these then select your final choices. Once you have made your selection you will receive high resolution headshots, colour corrected and cropped to the standard 10 x 8cm format.

Cost:

Adults £160 (with an added £10 if you choose to shoot outdoors). The package includes 350 images from which you can choose 4 to be retouched.

£120 for students, under 18s and over 65s (with £10 additional cost for outdoor shoot). The package includes

250 images from which you can choose 3 for retouching and finishing.

There is also a session for under 10s and it costs £80 for 30 minutes.

Website: https://davidjohnheadshots.com/

Location: Manchester- John Shard Studio, The Courtyard Studios, The Mews, Charlton Place, Ardwick Green, Manchester M12 6HS

London: 5 Torrens Street, Angel, London EC1V 1NQ

*Outdoor sessions in London are in Fitzrovia only. Further details upon request.

Email: davidjohnheadshots@gmail.com Tel: 07810 502424

Manchester Actors' Platform (MAP)

MAP offers affordable yet professional photo shoots providing you with high quality, colour and industry-ready headshots. The sessions are relaxed, and you can choose music if you like which does help you settle into your shoot and helps calm any nerves you might have. After a chat to find out a bit about you, what you want from your shoot and the roles you think you are right for, then you are ready to go. Your images will be narrowed down to 20-30 and you may select 3 for finishing and retouching. Bookings can be made directly from the website page below.

Cost: £75 (inclusive of VAT)

Website: https://www.maplatform.co.uk/headshots

Location: 53two Studios

Great Northern Warehouse, Unit 2, 235 Deansgate, Manchester M3 4EN

Phone: 07432 198724

Chris Keenan Photography

Chris works across the UK every week, so when you contact him to book your session you may be able to arrange a location that is close to you.

Each session costs £195 with a £50 deposit and the remaining £145 payable on the day of the shoot. Once you have decided on the headshots you prefer, the package includes 5 finished and retouched images which will be emailed over to you within 48 hours. Additional retouched images are charged at £25 each or, to receive the entire set of 150 images, (NOT RETOUCHED) £50.

The session lasts for up to 2 hours and Chris recommends 3 top changes in that time frame. Most of the shoots are done in natural light and Chris has several tried and tested locations across England. If you are not in England then do check with Chris via his online contact form on his website where the best location for you would be. He also has an indoor studio set up too if that is your preference.

Website https://www.chriskeenanheadshots.com/

Tel: 07917 524865

GETTING THE BEST FROM YOUR SHOWREEL

Along with a headshot you need to have a showreel to demonstrate your work. Casting directors want to see not only how you act, but also how you sound and move on camera. They have rapidly become an essential addition to an actor's profile on Spotlight and other casting websites.

I often hear the same question from actors who are starting out: 'but how can I get a showreel if I haven't done any television or film work?' I hope to be able to demystify this for you in the following section.

If you do have a speaking role on television then great, you can put it on your reel even if it is just a short piece. If your face can be seen and we can hear you and see you react, that is perfect. Many actors will get their first TV job playing roles such as police officers and nurses and these parts work perfectly to demonstrate your presence on camera. But what if you have never done any television or film work at all? There is more than one way around this so here are a few ideas for you to consider.

Bespoke Showreels

These are reels made for you by a showreel company (details of some are listed below). The company will write, film and edit a scene for you as part of the package. Some source locations, but do feel free to add your own ideas of places you know, and which don't involve expensive and time-consuming travel. Some companies supply costume and props depending on the type of scene you wish to film. Think about what type of character would suit you and ask the company to create a scene around this. I did one in which I played a hard-nosed police officer as it added a contrast to the softer, more caring roles that were already on my existing reel. This is another reason you need to know what you are selling and who you are as a PRODUCT. Make clear choices to give the director and writer of the reel. Have a look at the websites of various companies first to see the type of work they produce, because they can be quite varied, and consider the different genres they have done for other actors. Then either choose something that fits you, or suggest something new you would like to do. Make sure your scene gives you what you want from the character. You will be sent a draft script before your shoot date so be confident (not demanding) in your requirements. Pay attention and listen to the director; they will have shot a lot of reels and they know what they are talking about and what will sell you best. As a rule, you will be filming a duologue and you will need to find another actor to play against. (Top Tip – never work with an actor who is physically like you in looks, gender and age. It can be confusing for the viewer to understand which actor they are supposed to be watching). Casting directors work extremely quickly and may only watch 30 seconds of your reel, so you need to make an impact from the very start. It is quite widespread practice and a great idea to find another actor who also wants a reel made so you can share the cost. Turn up to your shoot day prepared and ready to work. Know your character, what you want from the day and, most of all, know your lines! Seems obvious, but it happens that actors sometimes don't. Monologues are not a great idea for your reel as a huge part of acting is listening and responding, so duologues are perfect. Theatre scenes don't really work either, as performances are bigger than for television and the sound will probably not be fit for purpose.

Your reel, once filmed, will then need your name, agent if you have one, and contact details added. It is usual practice for these to go at the end of the reel and they will be added by the company once you are happy with the edit. Never put music on the front of your reel and never do a montage of scenes. Most casting directors absolutely hate them. Your scene needs to be immediate, clear about who you are and who you are playing, show your presence on camera and how you listen and respond. A typical run time for your showreel, whether it be bespoke or made up of existing footage, should be no longer than 2 minutes and 20 seconds. This means you can upload it directly to Twitter and the entire reel will play automatically on your pinned Tweet. Also, there just isn't time in the casting suite to watch a long piece of work so you need to be disciplined about what you select. Make sure your best work is first and that it is current. There is no point in having old footage of when you were twenty years younger. Be honest with yourself and ask, 'would I really be cast in this role?'

Showreel companies are always happy to edit scenes of existing work you may have. They often offer advice on the scene order and what to leave out. They will always do their utmost to put the best and most impactful reel together for you. If you happen to be in a scene with a well-known actor, there is often a temptation to allow them camera time in your scene. Don't! Everyone knows their work, it's YOU that you are selling so get an edit where you are the focus.

Short Films

There is an ever-growing market for short films presently and they are becoming increasingly popular for both artists and viewers. There are many film festivals all over the world such as Sundance, which has a short film section, Raindance (Oscar, BAFTA and BIFA qualifying), Leeds International Film Festival, Kinofilm (Manchester), The London Short Film Festival, (LSFF), Aesthetica Short Film Festival (ASFF) and Cannes (short films under 15 mins only), to name just a few. You can, very often, find casting briefs for these films on Spotlight but if you don't yet have membership then check out Mandy.com which is a subscription service for casting information. (Details in the Casting Services section). Short films vary enormously thematically and stylistically, and you may get the opportunity to play a larger role, getting yourself and your work noticed. Pay a visit to short film festivals in and around your area to get an understanding of what is 'on trend' and to gain more of an insight into the type of work for which you would like to be considered. They are also a fantastic opportunity to network and meet film directors and producers. Be bold, hand them a copy of your CV.

Student Films

These are a fabulous way to get some on-set experience and showreel material at the same time. There are film schools in most parts of the country, and I have listed some below. Student films can be worth doing as they are often entered into film festivals nationally and internationally, so your work has the potential to be widely viewed. Personally, I prefer to do films for graduating students as their work is generally of a high standard and you need to have a good quality scene to add to your reel. This is just a personal preference, and you really can learn a lot from students wherever they are in their training. You will learn a lot of 'film speak' too on student films as well as getting the opportunity to work on technical skills such as 'hitting your mark', shot sizes etc.

Note

These days, there is an Equity agreement that covers the fees for working on student and short films, but make sure that you will receive a copy of the finished work. This is what you need for your reel so be clear about your agreement before you begin shooting. If you don't have an agent then make sure you have a clear understanding of what is expected of you. What are your call times? How are you to travel to the location? Are you insured? Are there any physical demands? Will they supply food on the shoot day? if you are working away from home, will accommodation be provided? Get everything down in writing. You need to protect yourself and be confident in having a fun and safe experience. This advice, of course, goes for any work you undertake as a self-represented performer and will be discussed more in the Personal Safety section of the book.

UK Film Schools

National Film and Television School. Locations in Beaconsfield, London, Leeds, Scotland and Wales.

https://nfts.co.uk/

London Film School

https://lfs.org.uk/

Leeds Beckett University, Northern Film School.

https://www.leedsbeckett.ac.uk/subjects/film/

University of York Theatre, Film, Television, Interactive Media

https://www.york.ac.uk/tfti/

Film and TV School Wales

SHOWREEL COMPANIES

Totally Showreels

Based in Leeds, Totally Showreels was created in 2012 to provide actors with high quality reels at affordable prices. Both Mike and Lee, who run the company, are actors, writers and directors, giving them first-hand experience of the demands and challenges you may face. Lee is also an acting teacher while Mike teaches media production and screenwriting. Totally Showreels can put together a customised reel for you from existing work or create a bespoke one from scratch.

Cost: All packages listed are fully bespoke. Scenes are written, produced, directed and edited based on the casting needs of the individual actor. After shooting, the edit is normally complete within two weeks, or earlier, and there is also help on how to upload your scene onto Spotlight.

Single Scene Package £270. Ideal for actors who wish to add a character or skill that is currently missing from their showreel.

Two Scene Package (most popular) £370. Two bespoke scenes filmed and edited to produce a complete showreel or add to existing footage.

Three Scene Package £470. Perfect for those of you with no existing footage at all. Three bespoke scenes that showcase character and skill variety.

Footage Editing from £50. Use your existing footage to create an interesting and engaging reel to catch the eye of agents and casting directors.

Contact: https://totallyshowreels.myportfolio.com/about-us for all details.

act4tv Group Showreel Shoot Sessions

Act4tv offers high quality group showreel shoot days for groups of 4 actors. The process begins with an in-depth consultation, after which the scene will be created for you based on your requirements. Once the script is finalised, you will be invited to attend a rehearsal prior to the confirmed shoot date. Each actor will prepare and shoot 2 scenes for their reel as well as partnering another actor for one of their scenes later in the day. Each actor will receive 2 fully graded and edited scenes. Turnaround to receive your reel is usually 14 days, and you can request one edit if needed. The cameras used for the shoot give cinematic quality footage found in commercial filming. Look at the website for examples of footage shot.

Website https://act4.tv/act4tv-productions/how-it-works/

Cost: £400 per actor (this rate is exclusive to act4tv members). A non- refundable deposit of £100 is required within 48 hours of booking to secure your place.

Location: Vernon Hill, Mersey Street, Stockport SK1 2HX.

Chris Stone Films

Chris is a Staffordshire based freelance director, offering bespoke showreels and showreel editing. A customised showreel scene which has been written, filmed and edited for you costs £430 per scene, not per actor, so you can share the cost with a friend. Before the shoot day, Chris will chat to you about your career so far, how you see yourself and where you want to work. He will then advise about what types of scripts and scenes would best show your skills. All scenes are duologues or monologues around 1.5 pages in length. You can also write your own scene if you prefer. You are responsible for finding any props, costumes and actors for your scene. Filming will take place in a location to which Chris has free access, with shooting taking around 3-4 hours per scene with a rehearsal, before heading out to the location. Once filming is completed, you will receive a first draft of the scene for feedback and approval. Chris will then apply any changes you want and send back the completed HD digital format showreel scene ready to upload to the internet and casting sites of your choice.

Check out the website to see examples of the showreels Chris has done for other actors and to view the FAQ section which will answer more of your questions.

Cost:

Custom filmed showreel scenes £430 (share the cost with another actor)

Packages: Standard £560 includes custom showreel scene, script and edit.

Silver £980 includes 2 filmed scenes, 2 scripts and the edit.

Gold £1,380 includes 3 filmed scenes, 3 scripts and the edit.

Website: https://www.chrisstoneshowreels.com/

Filmdock Productions

Based in London, Filmdock is a team of filmmakers with over 7 years' industry experience, including feature films, TV, documentaries and music videos. They offer high quality, bespoke, cinematic showreels for actors that look and sound great as well as showcasing your acting ability. Production values are high, with time spent in post-production to ensure you get everything you need from your showreel.

The first step is to have your consultation with the director and DP* for the shoot. This is completely free with no strings attached. This is where you can have an in-depth discussion about your needs, the roles you wish to play, your career to date and the type of reel you are looking for. You will also be made aware of the procedure on the day (locations, supporting actors etc). If you decide to go ahead, you can pay a deposit which is 25% of the package price. Once that has cleared, your booking is complete and you will be unable to cancel from that point. You can, however, reschedule your booking date. You will then be contacted by the script writer for your script consultation which will be done via Skype or Zoom. Be prepared for this meeting with specifics about the type of roles and characters you want to play as well as the scenarios you want the characters to be in. The more specific you are, the closer your script will be for your requirements. If you need help with ideas, look at the How to Pick a Scene video in the tips section of the Filmdock website. Be confident and honest; if there is something that you are not happy with, speak up. It is better to be clear at the outset rather than waste time later. After this consultation, the script writer will send you a brief for you to confirm and, once you have done so, they will write the script which normally takes a couple of days. You can still make MINOR changes at no extra cost, but anything that would require the script to be rewritten would incur additional payment. Filming a scene can take between 2-6 hours, including set up and rehearsal, depending on the package you choose. After filming, you will receive your fully edited showreel ready to upload to all the casting services within 10 working days.

*Director of Photography

Cost:

Bespoke showreels

New Hope Package - simplified scenes, essential coverage, only for showreel purposes.

1st Scene £279 (additional scenes shot on the same day £200)

Package includes pre-shoot consultation, bespoke script written of 1 page per scene.

Filming in 4K (up to 2 hours per scene on set).

Editing and sound mixing

Cinematic colour grading

10% - 50% off headshots.

The Rise Package – Standard show reel scenes, advanced coverage.

1st scene £349 (additional scenes filmed on the same day £225)

Pre shoot consultation.

Bespoke scripts written - 1.5-2 pages per scene.

Filming in 4K with up to 4 hours on set.

Location and scene partners are found if required.

Editing, sound mixing and design.

Music added (when appropriate)

Cinematic colour grading.

Free showreel editing.

20% - 50% off headshots

The Empire Package

Standalone scenes, full coverage, bigger crew, advanced preparation, more time on set.

£499 per scene

Pre-shoot consultations

Bespoke script written - 2.5-3 pages per scene. Script analysis session with the director.

Hair and makeup artist supplied

Filming in 4K with up to 6 hours on set.

Locations and scene partners found if needed.

Editing, sound mixing and design.

Music added (when appropriate)

Cinematic colour grading.

Free showreel editing

50% discount for headshots.

Note: Prices are charged per scene, not per actor so it might be cheaper to split the cost with someone else.

Headshot Sessions

 A standard headshot session lasts about 2 hours, and you will receive 3 retouched and finished images. After you session you will receive a digital contact sheet within 24 hours for you to select your images. After you send you choices back, you will get you completed headshots within 5 working days.

Cost: £160 for 3 images (£20 each for further images). Discounts are available if you book your showreel at the same time and full details are on the website.

Website: **https://filmdock.net/**

Email: contact form via the website.

Address: 47 Whetstone Road, London SE3 8PZ

CASTING DIRECTORIES AND SERVICES

If you have an agent, they will certainly be looking for work for you and putting you up for suitable roles, but you still need to be proactive and know what is going on. If you are currently unrepresented there are several reputable casting sites to which you can sign up. To get the complete service, they usually ask you to pay a fee and I have given details of these at the end of each listing. In most cases there is the option to pay monthly. You will be able to upload your headshots, showreel and CV. Be honest - never add a skill you can't deliver. I have heard stories of actors saying they can ride a horse, getting the job and then trying to find riding lessons before the shoot begins. It doesn't work and you will not be asked back. Check the sites daily to see if there is anything you are suitable for and then send sensible suggestions. There is no point applying if they are looking for someone who is exceptionally tall if you are 5 feet 1! Always check the dates of the shoot or the rehearsal and show dates to make sure that you are available for the full contract. Something that, quite rightly, bugs casting directors are actors who say they are available for a project who then announce they have to go to a wedding during the shoot or rehearsal period. Always be professional; if you miss out on this job then another one will surely come along. You need to make yourself fully aware of what will be expected of you; where you may need to travel, whether there will be food and accommodation, how much is the fee. A lot of casting briefs can be for low paid work, but if you feel that the quality is good then go for it; they are great for building your CV and for getting footage for your showreel. If you are in any doubt about a project, there is anything that makes you feel uncomfortable or you think is inappropriate, then report it to Equity. Never take a risk. Have a look online to see if you can find out more details about the production company and the type of work they do. Due diligence is essential, especially if you are representing yourself in the early days.

Spotlight

Established in 1927, Spotlight is the oldest and possibly the best-known casting service in the world. For decades, actors' details were published in giant volumes of the now iconic Spotlight Directories. Nowadays, everything is digital and entirely online. It is a complete service where you upload your headshots (up to 4 is recommended), your showreel, and voice demos. You can add up to 20 minutes of video in your media library and up to 20 minutes on your profile, so you can have more than one reel if you wish. Some actors may have a second for comedy, for example. You can also have up to 20 minutes of audio clips or voice reels on you profile and in your media library. There is a section for your CV where you can list all your skills and training.

There is also a jobs link page and, once you have uploaded your details, playing age and set your filters, you will receive emails direct to your inbox with a list of castings that are suitable for you. Once again, be selective in your submissions. If you don't have an agent, you can still be a Spotlight member and your entry will appear as 'c/o Spotlight' under your headshot.

To be accepted to Spotlight there are certain criteria you must fulfil. They are as follows for actors 18 plus.

You should have:

Named, paid speaking roles in 4 professional productions, not in pre- or post-production, in television, full length film, short films (on the BAFTA short film list), theatre productions or character-driven voice work. Qualifying credits DO NOT include commercials, idents, student films or any work as a supporting artist. Never supply false or inaccurate information as it may result in the removal of your page from the website. Each application is always assessed on its merits. Don't worry if you are unsuccessful the first time, you can always apply again and there are helpful advice contact numbers listed below if you want to chat to someone.

Young Performers

Must be represented by an agent and the agency should be registered with Spotlight.

Graduate Performers

To join Spotlight as a graduate member your course must meet a minimum criterion which is also endorsed by Equity UK. Applications for graduate entry open in the first term of your final year of professional training. A graduate membership is a one-off annual membership and you will automatically be invited to join Spotlight as a performer member after your graduating year is over. Not all schools are eligible, so check with Spotlight and the drama school you are considering.

What is expected of you as a Performer Member?

Correctly keep your profile up to date with current headshots and showreel footage.

Suggest yourself selectively for roles posted on the Spotlight Link.

Be polite and respectful to all industry professionals using the service including agents, casting directors and other performers.

If you have any queries regarding Spotlight membership email questions@spotlight.com

Or you can call the support team on 020 7437 7631.

There is a wealth of other information for actors on the Spotlight website such as advice and support, discounts, self-tape services, mental health and wellbeing, agents, room hire and much more.

Cost of Membership: from £162 per year.

Annual membership: for 18 plus £162

Young Performers: £106 age (4-25)

Graduate Members: £106

There is also an option to pay monthly by Direct Debit, if this suits you better, and all details can be found on the website or by contacting Spotlight directly. Discounts are available for deaf and disabled performers, who are also invited to join www.profileperformers.com which is a free video database service for actors and hosted by Spotlight and The National Theatre, designed to champion and promote deaf and disabled talent.

Contact Details: Spotlight,7 Leicester Place, London WC2H 7R

Website: www.spotlight.com

Tel: 020 7437 7631

Email: performers@spotlight.com

Mandy.com

First launched in 1996 as an online directory for finding work in film and television, its later incarnation, Casting Call Pro was created in 2004 and later merged with what is now Mandy.com in 2015. This is a large creative community of actors, theatre professionals, dancers, singers, voice artists musicians and extras. Like other casting websites, you can upload your headshots showreel, voice media and CV, although how much is visible depends on whether you are a premium member. If you have a free membership, you can upload one image and a single audio or showreel along with your CV. Paid memberships offer more and you will need a Premium Membership to apply for jobs. Once you sign up, you will receive emails with jobs matching your casting bracket. If you are a Premium Member, you can then apply using the online template and send your chosen headshot and CV with your showreel link. It is an easy system to use but, as always, be selective in your submissions. Once you have submitted, you can check the progress of your application and see if your media has been viewed and even if you have been shortlisted. If you are called in for a casting, you will receive an email via the platform. It is then up to you if you want to share your private details with the company as you continue. Many of the castings are for low-paid work, but it is an excellent way to start building your career and adding those all-important credits to your CV. There are, on occasion, some very lucrative jobs on there, so it is worth checking out daily.

There is also an actors' forum where you can ask questions and chat about the business. It is useful for picking up tips from other performers but be careful of using it as a platform to vent about your lack of auditions, your agent (or lack of one). Stay professional and be positive.

Contained within the website there is a handy services directory where you can find information on agents, casting directors, film and television companies.

Premium Membership.

Annual Subscription: £130 with a £31 discount for full payment, so you will pay £99 in total.

Monthly Subscription: £17 + tax where applicable (auto renews every month until you cancel).

Website: https://www.mandy.com

Backstage

Backstage has been around for over 50 years and has a membership of over 100,000. As a member, you can create your talent profile and have access to unlimited applications. You can upload unlimited media. The site has a search feature, so it really narrows down the roles that are suitable for you, saving a lot of time. If theatre is not your thing, you can simply uncheck that box and those castings will not be sent to you. Type of castings you might typically find on Backstage are for commercials, voice over work, short and independent films and extra work. There are also calls for influencers and content creators and models. NOTE: Mandy and Backstage are now part of the same family and share the same account credentials. While both services are still separate and post their own castings and opportunities, you can use your Mandy password to access your Backstage account.

Website: https://www.backstage.com/casting/

Cost:

Annual fee of £84.99

Six-month membership £49.99

Monthly membership £14.99

StarNow

Conceived by three Kiwi expats in 2004 to help actors find work, their goal was to connect performers to casting professionals and to allow them to apply for castings. StarNow is open to every age, ethnicity, location and level of experience and is utilized by actors just starting out to pros who are more established in the industry. It has evolved massively over the years and now hosts work for actors, presenters, dancers, singers, musicians, influencers and extras. StarNow has more than 4 million members worldwide with a dominant market presence in UK, Australia and New Zealand as well as growing numbers of members in Canada, USA, Ireland and South Africa.

Actors can sign up for free and create a basic profile that highlights your skills, interests and experience. You are then able to search for all jobs that suit your casting bracket and type. There is a trial membership which offers you a basic profile upload and opportunity to apply for a limited number of castings.

For a monthly fee, you can upgrade and apply directly for unlimited auditions and jobs, appear in the talent directory and add more photos, video and audio to your profile.

When you create your profile, you add your location using the drop-down menu and jobs in that area appear. So, for example, if you are a female actor from Liverpool age 23-29, only relevant jobs will come up for you and they do vary in quality and type from area to area. Some castings accept applications from all over the UK and this is stated at the bottom of the listing. You can also choose to uncheck any jobs that are unpaid. Paid work is highlighted in green next to each casting. (Note: StarNow is not an agency and does not guarantee work. You will communicate directly with directors or producers on all aspects of the job including pay, invoices etc).

Website: https://www.starnow.co.uk/

Cost:

£4.99 per month for 6 months (save 58%)

£9.99 per month for 3 months (save 17%)

£11.99 monthly

Dramanic

A UK based casting website with information on auditions for London and Regional Theatre. Launched in 2011, Dramanic is aimed at helping the professional actor find work in theatre throughout the UK. (**Note: you do need to be professionally trained and be working to be eligible for this site).**

When you sign up you will automatically get a two-week free trail after which you can opt to upgrade and use the paid site. Features include personalised CV and business card, dedicated, actor-focused emails direct to your inbox, a casting calendar highlighting audition opportunities, a comprehensive database of casting directors, theatre companies and agents, a useful self-employed tax guide for actors, swap plays / books with other site users and some non-acting job listings for actor-friendly work when you are in between jobs.

Website: https://www.dramanic.com/uk/

Cost:

Cheapest £116.99 for 12 months

Affordable £65.99 for 6 months

Popular £40.99 for 3 months

Taster £14.99 for 1 months

Casting Networks

Casting Networks is a sophisticated casting platform, created in the USA, which allows you to search and apply for jobs directly, upload your headshot, showreel and voice media and attach links to your online CV, so everything is in one place.

You can opt for a basic membership or upgrade to premium which will give you unlimited media uploads and to submit to any project listed on the casting site. A basic membership lets you upload your first 2 photos, video clip and an audio clip free of charge as well as search for jobs. You will have to upgrade to a premium membership to submit yourself. For more information and to contact Casting Networks, please see their website.

https://www.castingnetworks.com/

Act On This

Although Act on This is not really a casting website as such, it is a hugely useful platform for any actor starting out as well as those already working in the business and keen to make a bigger impact in their careers.

Created by Ross Grant with the aim of empowering actors and giving them the confidence and knowledge of how the industry works, Act on This offers weekly online coaching with established industry professionals. Members get access to 7 online sessions a month for £24. If you can't attend a live broadcast, there is a replay available, so you never miss out. Previous webinars have been hosted by 'Line of Duty' casting director Daniel Edwards, 'Brassic' co-creator Danny Brocklehurst and head of 'Hollyoaks' casting Peter Hunt. There are many more to which you can gain access once you sign up. You will also find over 100 hours of videos and podcasts with advice from casting directors and other industry professionals as well as monthly group networking and 1-1 coaching sessions all included in the membership package. You will also be able to join the community forum to share ideas, get recommendations on photographers or find someone to read in for your self-tape.

Packages and prices are as follows:

Monthly £24 (subject to change). Cancel anytime, no minimum contract.

Package includes:

4 live mastermind calls every month.

2 group Q&A calls every month.

1 networking call every month.

Recordings of all mastermind calls.

100 hours of videos and podcasts with industry professionals.

24/7 community forum access.

Invitations to exclusive industry workshops

Act On This iPhone and Android App.

Yearly: £247 (with £344 in bonuses)

All the same offers as the monthly package + these bonuses

Social Media Deep Dive - training for actors.

A comprehensive and up to date database of agents and casting directors which is updated quarterly.

Contact:

Website https://www.actonthis.tv/

Email help@actonthis.tv

APPROACHING AN AGENT

Time to pause and take a moment's reflection on where you are now. Have you found the school where you wish to train and are you being consistent in your attendance? Have you got a headshot and showreel you are happy with, and have you done some work either on screen or in the theatre to build your credits? Do you know what you are selling? Are you clear on the roles you see yourself playing and the trajectory you imagine your career taking? An understanding of these things is vital before thinking of approaching an agent. They get hundreds of letters asking for representation every week, so you need to stand out as being professional, well-prepared and knowledgeable about the business.

The best time to approach an agent is when you are doing something such as a show. They need to see you work and, although a good showreel might be enough to get you taken on, there is no substitute for watching you perform live. It proves your ability to maintain a performance throughout the journey of a play, as well as allowing agents to see how you move, what you sound like and what your physical presence is like. So, if you are in a show, send an invite to your chosen agencies, giving plenty of notice of the dates. If you have a television or film role, alert them to the transmission and date and ask them to have a look, again giving plenty of notice.

So now let's look at the best practice to make that all important approach for representation.

Note: Never pay an agent to be on their books!

No reputable agency will ever ask for money upfront. If they do, politely decline and inform Equity.

Do your research. There are directories listed in this book where you can find contact details of agents. **Contacts**, published by Spotlight is an excellent resource which is updated annually. Begin by looking at the agency website and checking out their client list. If you see an actor who is an obvious clash with your type and skill set, then it is probably not worth applying. Look at the CVs of the actors on an agent's books and see what kind of work they have been doing. If it is something you would like to do, then mention it in your cover letter. In the contact section of the website there will always be instructions on how to apply for representation – make sure you follow them. Don't limit yourself to smaller agents just because you are starting out. Some of the bigger names in the business will still represent you if you have a particular look, skill, or talent they like. Make a shortlist of the agents who have actors doing the kind of work you would prefer. Be selective in your choices. There is no point just blanketing across the industry. It will take forever, and you are unlikely to find yourself represented by the best agency for you.

The Cover Letter

This is hugely important and must not be overlooked. It is your first introduction to an agent even before they see your headshot so make sure it is clear, concise and with correct spelling. Have you addressed it to the right person? It takes time to find out the names of the agents within an agency, but it is courteous to do so. Never just write 'dear agent,' or copy and paste your letters. They need to be personal and well-thought-out giving precise reasons why you want to join their client list. There is no need to write a life story. Your CV and photo speak for themselves. Introduce yourself and say why you would like to be represented by the agency. Mention that you like the work of certain actors on their books and say where you see yourself in the next couple of years. It might be a good idea to highlight where you are based and if you have other bases away from home, and mention if you are appearing in anything they can watch. No need to send large files of images. Simply add your Spotlight link if you have one or a link to your showreel. All applications are read and seriously considered but there are simply too many for agents to be able to reply, unless they are interested and want to talk further, in which case they will call you in for a meeting. Don't pester them. Let it go, and if after a year or so, you are working and still want them to be your agent, you can invite them to see you. But never be desperate. Move on to the next one. Rinse and repeat.

Building your relationship

So, fast forward to the now represented you. How do you manage your relationship with your agent? Primarily, always be polite and professional. You and your agent are a team and you need to be able to work well together. This means letting them know if you are not available because of holidays, weddings, funerals, hospital appointments etc. It is a nightmare for all concerned if you get a casting or a job offer only for you to announce you're off on holiday for a week. Most agencies are linked to TAGMIN, the online calendar so you can update it with any dates you will not be free. You can also add skills to your profile. Since the pandemic, there is an option for you to upload your COVID19 vaccination status. Lots of production companies will not allow you to work without at least a double vaccination so this might be something you need to discuss with your agent.

When your agent sends through a casting brief, read it carefully. Are you happy you want to do the job? Don't be tempted to go for the audition if you don't want the job or know you won't be available. Be honest. If it's not for you, that's fine but you must be clear. If you wish to go ahead with a casting, make sure you know exactly what is expected of you. What do they want in your self-tape? What is the deadline? Where is the location of your meeting? Any questions should be asked well in advance of the audition day, so you are not stressed, and neither is your agent.

Once you are offered a role, your agent will negotiate your fee to get the best for you. They will draw up your contract and likely do some social media shout-outs for you. NEVER mention a job on social media before your contract is signed. To be on the safe side, it's best to wait and let your agent do it for you. Commission is a standard 10% for theatre and 15% for television work. This might vary, depending on the agency but they will tell you this when they take you on and it will be clearly stated in the terms of your contract.

Staying in touch

There is no need to call your agent daily. Maybe check-in via email once a month to see what they have put you up for and, of course, you can call if you have any worries or questions. Arrange a catch-up meeting once or twice a year but don't be a pest. Rest assured, they will be working for you so be patient. And remember to say thanks! I'm not intending to be patronising here, but it is so easy to do and so easy not to do. Expressing gratitude for the time and effort that has gone into getting you a job should be standard.

If things don't work out

Sometimes, things just don't work out, and you decide to move on to pastures new. A standard contract generally allows an actor to leave an agency after giving one month's notice of intention to leave. You cannot change your Spotlight details to that of your new representation until this time has elapsed. This is to avoid confusion about who to pay commission to in the event of you being offered a role during your notice period. Once you have decided to move on, call or write to your agent explaining your decision. Never lay blame at their door and don't complain about them afterwards. It's a small business and word gets round.

TOP TIP: resist the tendency to jump around from agent to agent if you are having a dry spell. It is rarely your agent's fault if you are not working. It is the business and part of it is having the fortitude and resilience to keep going. Talk to them if you are having doubts. A quick catch-up over a cup of tea can do wonders to alleviate fears and prevent you from jumping ship when it's not necessary.

If you need more professional advice of finding and approaching an agent, then contact Spotlight on:

Tel: 020 7437 7631

Email: performers@spotlight.com

CONTACTING CASTING DIRECTORS (CDs)

Sending emails out to casting directors can seem like a thankless task. You will rarely receive a reply or acknowledgment but do not despair. CDs receive hundreds of unsolicited submissions from actors, and it would be impossible for them to reply to everyone, but rest assured, they will look at your details. The demands of the business mean they must work quickly which is another reason your headshot must stand out. Do your research first. You can find details of CDs online, so take the time to look at the type of productions they have recently cast. Make a note of anything you particularly enjoyed as you can mention it in your cover letter. Pay attention to the genre in which they work, for example, if a CD specializes only in casting children and young people, don't bother contacting them if you are an adult actor. The same rules as always apply; know who you are, be disciplined and selective in who you contact.

Your cover letter should be concise, to the point and polite. No long rambling stories about how much you have always wanted to be on TV or how hard-working you are. Stick to the relevant information. If a series set in Yorkshire is being cast, for example, and you are from that area, that is a good time to reach out. Highlight your native accent, where you were born and are based. Likewise, it is worth mentioning if you have a special skill that suits a production. Don't send large files with your headshot or showreel as they will probably not be opened. If you are on Spotlight, it is enough to add your link at the bottom of the email. If you are not yet a member, then send your CV as a PDF or Word Document.

Invite CDs to see you work if you are in a show but as with agents, give plenty of notice of dates.

Don't overdo it though. Staying in touch is fine but isn't necessary to write every week or month. If anything relevant changes, such as you add new showreel footage or get new headshots, then it is ok to contact but no more than once every six months. CDs have brilliant memories and if something suitable comes up, they will remember you. It is a good idea to find out how a CD prefers to be contacted. They will usually say on their website, so follow the rules. Generally, email is the most acceptable method of contact. Don't phone or visit the office. There are tales of maverick actors making bold moves and scoring a life changing role, but they are very rare so don't do it. Being an actor is a business and, like all businesses, it needs to be run professionally.

NOTES

AUDITIONS

Hurray! You've successfully bagged an audition. What to do next?

First, check the details on the brief you have received with a fine-tooth comb. Where and when is the audition? Are you available for the meeting and for the dates of the job? What are you required to do regarding character, accents etc? Make sure that you are happy with all the information before you continue. Any questions? Then this is the time to ask. Check with your agent or the CD if you are unsure about anything. Then you need to research the director, theatre, show or programme you are up for. This gives you the opportunity to find out what the director has been doing and, more importantly, what their style is. If you view their showreel and see that they favour a Mike Leigh style of realistic performance, then that is probably what you will be expected to do in the room or for your casting. Find out what the CD has recently worked on; again, it gives you an idea about them, shows you are interested and is a talking point in the audition room.

Be fully prepared with your script printed or stored on an iPad if you prefer. Read the script a few times, then make a note of the location of the scene. Is it day or night? Who are the characters and what is their relationship? Look for the FACTS in the scene. What do you know? Highlight them, they tell you a lot about the character What do other people say about the character? Study the punctuation it can also give clues as to how a character might be feeling in a given moment. Let's imagine that your scene is set in a hospital corridor late at night. The character is a young medical professional who has made a mistake and is trying to cover their tracks. How will they speak? Loudly or quietly? What is their body language like? Who is around them that could overhear? Build a complete picture of the story BEFORE you begin learning the lines. Giving a context and geography to a scene is half of the work and makes your performance believable and natural.

If you are in the room for your meeting, make sure you arrive on time. Things can go wrong with transport and, if this happens, make sure that you have all the contact numbers you need so you can let the CD know you are running late. Try not to arrive all flustered. Take a bottle of water and take a moment to calm yourself. Look at the script and if you need a bit more time then it is, within reason, perfectly acceptable to ask for a few minutes longer to prepare.

Enter the room with confidence. No need to shake hands with everyone. Listen carefully to any questions you are asked and the explanation of the play or programme. Again, any questions then ASK. This is **your** audition. Be natural and friendly. This chat is designed to allow the director to see your personality and assess how you will be to work with. If you are nervous, it's not a problem. If you are dyslexic or have any access requirements or additional needs, then do flag them up. The director and CD are used to this and will accommodate you in every way they can.

You will be asked to read the script, sometimes with another actor reading in for you or sometimes with the CD. After the first read, this is where you may be given some direction. Listen carefully to the notes and do your best to deliver what has been asked of you. They are looking at how well you take direction as well as how collaborative you are. Try to think of your audition as an opportunity to perform and play rather than a job interview. It makes you more relaxed and lessens any sense of desperation which is never a good energy to bring into the room. Once the meeting has ended thank the panel, and leave. Do not loiter around after. If you see someone you know, and want to go for a coffee afterwards, wait outside for them. Keep the whole procedure clean, efficient and professional.

Now for the hard part. The waiting. I'm not sure that this gets any easier with experience, but you have to let it go and get on with life. Some actors like to throw the script away as soon as they leave the audition room as a gesture of release. The Yes / No Campaign, of recent years, has helped somewhat in letting actors know if they have been successful, but the truth is you might never hear back. It's not great but it is part and parcel of the job, and you have to learn to manage it in the way that works for you. Look at the section on Your Mental Health and Wellbeing for tips on how to manage expectations, rejection etc. Stay positive Auditioning is a learning curve, too, and the more you do, the better at it you will become.

SELF-TAPES

Self-tapes are now a seemingly permanent part of the post lockdown world and much of what has been said regarding in the room auditions holds true.

The same rules apply for preparation. Read the brief fully, make sure you understand what is needed from you and prepare your script in the same way you would for a face-to-face meeting.

With self-tapes, however, pay great attention to the instructions sent from the CD on the brief. They will send you a character breakdown and may suggest what to wear. If this is not stated, then use your initiative. If the character is a barrister then dress to give sense of the role. No need to source a full wig and gown.

Look carefully for the deadline for your tape and make sure you adhere to it. There can be quick turnarounds for submissions, especially for commercials and, if you can't reasonably deliver your tape, let your agent or the CD know. They may be able to give you an extension and it makes everyone's life easier if they don't have to chase you up, only then to find that you can't deliver. As there is more of a move towards paperless offices, you may find that the documentation you need to complete is also within the brief via a link to the online casting sheet. Here you will have to complete your details such as agent, contact number, height and measurements. You will also have to upload a current headshot and list any commercials you have done in the last 3 years. Be mindful of your headshot and send the one which best represents the role you are up for. Follow the instructions **to the letter** on how the tapes should be labelled and transferred. Send them as an MP4 as these can be downloaded onto most computers. So, for example, if the instructions say 'please label your tape, name, role and agent', that is all you need to do. The CD may wish to receive the tape via WeTransfer or similar method and, again, do exactly as they ask. If you are sending your tape to your agent for checking, then follow the same instructions. They will be downloading numerous tapes every day and it really helps speed up the process if everything is labelled and formatted correctly. You will have to compress your tape before sending, as large files take far too long to download. There are apps available to do this. Some are free and others charge a fee.

For the technical side of the tape, there are several excellent and affordable online workshops which give you the advice you need to record, edit and send an acceptable tape. This will include details on compressing your tape and how to transfer it.

Briefly, tapes can be filmed on a phone, iPad, laptop, or video camera if you have one. You need to tape against a blank background; no clutter or personal objects should be in the shot. A grey wall is ideal, but don't feel the need to rush out and buy a tin of paint. A plain white background is also fine, as are other colours, but make sure that there is a contrast between what you are wearing, hair colour etc. If you have dark hair, work against a lighter background so that you stand out. You can buy a photographic backcloth fairly cheaply. CDs need to be able to see and hear you, so your sound and lighting need to be good. Natural light is fine, but remember that it can change and sudden cloud coverage could ruin an excellent take. You can buy soft boxes which are probably the best option. Avoid ring lights, if possible as they leave circles in your eyes resulting in a slightly alien effect which is distracting. In terms of sound, this can be tricky as life will be going on around you as you work. Make sure there are no fridges or other household appliances humming in the background. If your neighbour is playing loud music, best to wait until it has stopped before you begin recording. Use the time to prepare and rehearse. I lived in a house for many years with geese outside and working between the noise they made was a mission, but it is possible with patience and perseverance. Lav mics are available online and they might help cancel out some ambient noises.

For your editing, iMovie is excellent and easy to use as is Climpchamp where you can compress and change the format of your tape. I have listed the classes, equipment and technical platforms I find work well below.

If you want a comprehensive workshop on self-taping, check out **Manuel Puro's 21 Day Self-Tape Challenge**. Scripts are sent out every evening at 7pm and you have until 7pm the following day to rehearse, record, edit and post your tape. There are also advice sessions and webinars with Manuel where he explains the technical elements of self-taping and gives feedback on the work you have submitted. Details below.

Mixing Networks runs online and live workshops in London. There are 3 levels. Everyone must begin and complete level 1, whatever their experience, before they can move on to the next stage. Again, the courses are detailed and comprehensive. Scripts are sent for you to prepare, record and upload. At level 1 you will receive feedback and technical advice. You then resubmit the same scene the following week including the notes you were given to gauge improvement. Details of workshops below.

https://www.purocasting.com/the-acting-habit/the-21-day-self-tape-challenge

https://mixingnetworks.com/

https://clipchamp.com/en/

Equipment: Soft Box lights, Lav Mic, Tripod Stand, Photographic Cloth for the background. These are just suggestions and tapes can still be made if you don't have this equipment.

ROLE PLAY WORK

There may be times when you are not working as an actor and are looking for another job to keep the money coming in. Working as a role player is a great option as it can be quite lucrative and it allows you to practice your skills, as you will be working in character, often improvising around a scenario which has been sent to you in advance. The main types of role play work are Medical and Corporate.

Medical role play is booked through an agency or the communication skills office of a university. It requires you to thoroughly learn a script containing the medical and social history of the person you are playing. Roles are cast according to playing age. Briefings are sent out and training given before each session to prepare you for the day. If you are booked for an exam day you will be expected to travel to the hospital where they are being held. Be prepared. The days are very long and require a lot of stamina and attention to detail. Every encounter must be the same as the previous one to ensure fairness throughout the exam. You may have upwards of 48 encounters per day. These can be emotionally challenging so don't take on work that is close to a personal situation and make sure you do something fun and nice for yourself at the end of the day.

Corporate role play, on the other hand, is very different. It is often high end and you are expected to be extremely well prepared for the work. A brief will be sent which must be thoroughly learned. You may be asked to participate in some Forum Theatre, where you will play various scenes demonstrating best and worst practice, then facilitate breakout sessions where you will run bespoke role play encounters. Accurate feedback is then given by the role player to aid developmental learning for each delegate. Areas for corporate work include, finance, health and safety, telecommunications and recruitment. Your personal presentation must be professional so it is worth investing in a business outfit in order to look the part. The money can be very good for these jobs and there is often the opportunity to travel regionally and abroad.

Role Play companies across the country can be found via a Google search but here are one or two to give you an idea of how they operate. As you begin to work in this area, create a CV that is separate to your acting resume as you may be asked to send it as part of an application for an agency.

Medical Role Play Companies

Role Play North (School of Medical Education, Newcastle University)

https://www.ncl.ac.uk/sme/engagement/roleplaynorth/

Medical Role Players (Nationwide)

https://www.medicalroleplayers.co.uk/

email medicalrolepalyers@gmail.com

PRP Medical Role Play (Nationwide)

https://www.prplayers.co.uk/

Corporate Role Play Companies

Role Plays for Training (Book actors for role play work nationwide)

https://rpft.uk/

Peel Entertainment (Role Play Work as well as opportunities for performers)

https://www.peeltalent.com/

YOUR MENTAL HEALTH AND WELLBEING

There is no doubt that being a performer can be mentally tough. You will face rejection, disappointment and periods of being out of work. Here are some tips to help keep you mentally healthy and strong. Some I have learned the hard way and others have come to me through various practices I have found along the road. Make a habit or routine of the suggestions that work for you, and they will serve you well. It does take a degree of discipline but like everything, the rewards are worth it.

Create a Routine

The industry is, by its very nature, unpredictable and can lead to prolonged periods of unemployment. Therefore, it is fundamental to create a solid routine and stick to it to feel a sense of stability and progress in your life. Plan your day the night before. Make a note of 6 things you want to achieve the next day, so you have an automatic focus when you get up. Cross off the things you have done. Crossing stuff off lists is incredibly pleasing and gives a sense of achievement. If you don't manage to get everything done that day, don't beat yourself up about it. Simply move that activity to the following day and prioritise it for then. Activities could include an exercise routine, drafting emails, doing research online, applying for castings. Give yourself a time period. It may be that you are working in a day job or have other commitments and this can help you to fit everything in more comfortably. So, for example, if you get up at 8.00am, plan to finish your activities, by, say 11.00am so that you have the rest of the day to do other things. Create a timetable that suits your commitments and follow it Monday - Friday. At the end of the week, look at your lists and you will see just how much you have achieved -

you will be amazed and, hopefully, feel positive and successful. Make sure to do something outside of the business too. Hobbies are a great way of relaxing and letting go of anxiety as you put your focus into something else.

Take Breaks

Busy schedules can take their toll on physical and mental wellbeing. We often find ourselves being busy for the sake of being busy. We can't manage time, but we can manage our activities within it. Make sure you take breaks. Get some fresh air, meet a friend for a coffee, go and sit in the park. It's important to clear you mind and get some perspective on the situation. It is so easy to get locked into a thought pattern that isn't serving us other than to make us feel bad, so schedule some free time. Maybe work in blocks of 60-minute sprints then do something else. Stretch, move and take deep breaths.

Change your Perspective

Perspective is your way of looking at things, your point of view and it can be changed. The way we look at something can have an enormous impact on how we feel. It generates thoughts that can often be negative and these, in turn, cause negative feelings to arise. Switch it up, if you're feeling low because you haven't had a casting or because you are broke, focus on what you DO have. Make a list of all the positives you have in your life and give gratitude for them. It sounds simple and it is, but it's a game changer. Make a daily habit of doing this to see the best results.

Meditation and Mindfulness

Mindfulness is the practice of simply noticing what is going on around you. It is about being present, in the

NOW. When we look into the future, it can often attract worries and doubt about how we will manage things. We begin to imagine all sorts of scenarios that haven't happened, and this can lead to catastrophizing. Living in the past can potentially take you down the route of regret and self- doubt: 'why didn't I do that in the audition?' 'I should have worn that outfit'. Let it go! Focus on what is happening now. Concentrate on your breath and feel it entering and leaving the body. Feel the air on your skin, hear the noises around you. When you go for a walk, if you can, notice the birds and the trees. Thoughts will jump back into your head, that's what the mind does but once you notice them, you can change them. Mental muscles work in the same way as physical ones when you go to the gym. You can't go once and then have a beautiful, toned body. You have to repeat the exercise frequently. So it is with the mind. Mental chatter takes a while to calm, so be patient with yourself. There is a great series of books by Danny Penman which are worth checking out. They come with meditations and exercises to follow.

Mindfulness in a Frantic World by Danny Penman.

Don't compare yourself with others

In this age of social media and 24-hour connection, this is a temptation hard to resist. Scrolling through Instagram or Twitter and comparing yourself with others can impact thoughts negatively. We look at how well everyone else seems to be doing and wonder where we went wrong. Why is my career not as glitteringly successful as theirs? I see lots of posts by actors saying they are doing a self-tape, are on their way to a casting or have just booked an amazing job. Yes, social media is an incredibly useful tool for finding out about castings, events and classes but try to use it just for that. It is a lot easier said than done and I still fall into the trap of allowing the things I read to affect me, but there are ways to limit the impact, such as reducing your time online. Check your social media feeds maybe only twice a day maximum to make sure that you're not missing something important but, otherwise, no scrolling through other actors' accounts, wondering why they are having all the luck. Instead, use the time wisely and do something initiative-taking towards your own goal. Book a class, do some self-tape practice, or read a play or autobiography. Work out the amount of time per day you spend scrolling and then either do something career orientated or something completely different with that time instead. It's a win-win situation and really goes a long way to stop the negative chatter in the mind. Be kind to yourself. Buy yourself a little treat at the end of the week. A coffee, cake or pay for something you enjoy. Relax, just be you and have fun!!

PERSONAL SAFETY

It is with a sense of regret that I must end the book on this note. However, sometimes things are not what they first seem and so here are a few words of advice to help avoid potentially challenging situations.

I must confess that I have taken risks with my personal safety. I went to auditions at the houses of directors, I travelled across the country without due diligence of the production I was auditioning for and yes, I found myself in a couple of tricky situations. I would like to think that we live in more enlightened times regarding safeguarding and having the confidence to voice our preferences and personal boundaries but, unfortunately, there are still those out there who feel they have the right to exploit people.

There are a lot of websites which offer castings and while most of them are well-monitored and reputable, it is not impossible for something inappropriate to slip through even the best run and well-established platform. If you are unrepresented, it is your job to be diligent. If you see something that looks wrong or makes you feel uncomfortable then flag it up. Contact the actors' union Equity and let them know. They do an excellent job at following up these complaints, as does Spotlight if something is flagged from their site.

If you have set yourself up with an audition, make sure to meet in a public space. Theatre cinema and arts centre coffee bars are a good option. It is very unlikely that a reputable director or producer will contest this. If they do then treat it as a red flag.

Inappropriate language, (including racism, sexism, homophobia, transphobia, or discriminatory comments about disability) is unacceptable and should be reported to the correct channels. There are union agreements for nudity, and these must be strictly adhered to. You will NEVER be asked to audition while undressed in any circumstances in a genuine casting. Your agent or the CD will let you know it is part of the role and you can give your consent to proceed. Everything is clearly stated, and you can find further information by contacting Equity (details below). If you are represented, then get in touch with your agent.

https://www.equity.org.uk/

FINAL WORD

I hope you have found the information in this book useful. Some of the details will change as time goes on so it is my intention to update the book annually. The suggestions I have made are for your guidance only. Try things out. Not everything will resonate with you, but I hope that this helps you on your first steps to following your dream.

You deserve success so go out and make it happen and remember….

'You didn't come this far, only to come this far.'

With love to you all.

Good luck.

RECOMMENDED READING

Respect for Acting by Uta Hagen

The Art of Acting by Stella Adler

Year of the King by Antony Sher

Beside Myself by Anthony Sher

On the Technique of Acting by Michael Chekhov

USEFUL ORGANISATIONS

British Actors' Equity

https://www.equity.org.uk/

Spotlight

https://www.spotlight.com/

Clipchamp for Video Editing

https://clipchamp.com/en/

Manuel Puro 21 Day Challenge

https://www.purocasting.com/the-acting-habit/the-21-day-self-tape-challenge

Printed in Poland
by Amazon Fulfillment
Poland Sp. z o.o., Wrocław

89085725R00069